Milestones Into Headstones

12-25-87

Merry Christmas!

for Ben who is a
fountain of the information
like that included in this
book — tell us all about it ...

love,

David &
Sherman

Every calling is great when greatly pursued.
Oliver Wendell Holmes, Jr.

Milestones
INTO Headstones

Mini Biographies of Fifty Fascinating Americans Buried in Washington, D.C.

PETER EXTON and DORSEY KLEITZ

EPM Publications, Inc.
McLean, Virginia

Copyright © 1985 Peter Exton and Dorsey Kleitz
All rights reserved
Printed in the United States of America
EPM Publications, Inc., 1003 Turkey Run Road, McLean, Virginia 22101

Book and cover design by Susan Lehmann

Library of Congress Cataloging in Publication Data
Exton, Peter.
Milestones into headstones.
   1. United States—Biography. 2. Washington (D.C.)—
Biography. 3. Burial—Washington (D.C.) I. Kleitz,
Dorsey. II. Title.
CT215.E98 1985 920'.073 85-13097
ISBN 0-914440-84-5

The book's title comes from these lines written by James Russell Lowell on his 68th birthday:

As life runs on, the road grows strange
With faces new, and near the end
The milestones into headstones change,
'Neath every one a friend.

Pictured on the front cover (from upper left to lower right) are: Phil Sheridan, Helen Keller and Annie Sullivan, William Jennings Bryan, William Howard Taft, Constantino Brumidi, Robert Ingersoll, George Dewey.
On the back cover are: Joe Louis, Simon Newcomb, Vinnie Ream, John F. Kennedy, Edwin M. Stanton, Medgar Evers, Oliver Wendell Holmes, Jr.

To Ellen and Sandy

A Note on the Suggested Reading

We hope some of our readers may be inspired by our mini-biographies to look deeper into the lives of these fascinating Americans. With that in mind, we have followed each sketch with suggestions for further reading. Most suggestions are full-length biographies selected for reliability of the material and appeal to the general reader.

For those who must have more, the Library of Congress is a good place to look. Diaries, letters, and other personal papers of many of our subjects are preserved in the Library's Manuscript Division. A variety of graphic materials can be found in the collections of the Prints and Photographs Division.

P.E., D.K.

Contents

Acknowledgments

Our Special Thanks to

the staffs of the Library of Congress, National Archives, Smithsonian Institution, National Portrait Gallery, Columbia Historical Society, and the Alexandria, Fairfax, and Arlington County Libraries.

Dolores Peterson of Arlington National Cemetery.

Helen Yost of the Licking County (Ohio) Historical Society.

Inge Baum of the House of the Temple, Scottish Rite Supreme Council.

Roxanna Deane of the Washingtoniana Division, Martin Luther King Memorial Library.

Cathy Novelli, for her generosity and patience.

If Tombstones Could Talk

Exploring Washington, D.C. is like rummaging through a treasure chest of America's past. Enter the door to any one of the city's museums, galleries, and public buildings and you plunge into the richness of our national heritage. Our history, science, technology, natural beauty, and fine arts are all reflected here and much of it, preserved in one way or another.

The museums are brimming with so many material things, however, that we run a risk of overlooking or forgetting the people who made these things worth seeing. To be sure, it is much easier to display a rig like the *Spirit of St. Louis* than to bring to life the story of Charles Lindbergh. But that bolted box of wire and metal will never be as exciting as the man who flew it. He gave it meaning. In making his transatlantic flight, Lindbergh created the historic moment that the airplane only represents.

We wrote this book because we believe that the people who shaped our history and created its artifacts are more important and usually far more interesting than the artifacts themselves. We wanted in effect to produce something like a museum collection of fascinating Americans. There are thousands of men and women who qualify, and choosing among them was an impossible task. We discovered, however, that a kind of pre-selection had been made for us. It lay right at our feet on the headstones in the cemeteries of Washington.

Since its birth as our national capital in 1800, Washington has become not only the most important city in the world, it has become America's most prominent resting place as well. More Americans who shaped and colored our national life are buried here than in any other area of the country. The 50 persons we finally chose for our collection were nearly all linked in some way with the official life of the capital.

Our 50 came from all walks of life and made their mark in a wide range of activities. The names of many are known in every school and home; some, unfortunately, have long been overlooked. Many were brilliant, and a few were just "regular folks" who made the most of their abilities. One, the indomitable Peggy Eaton, paralyzed social and political Washington simply by being herself.

Oliver Wendell Holmes, Jr., himself one of our selectees, believed that "it is required of a man that he should share in the passion and action of his time at peril of being judged not to have lived." Every man and woman chosen for this book fulfilled Holmes's requirement. They include such persons as:

• Alexander Gardner, an immigrant from Scotland who came to America to live in a utopian commune and wound up photographing some of the most haunting scenes of the Civil War.

• Vinnie Ream, a resolute teenage sculptor whose first attempt in marble is the full-size statue of Abraham Lincoln that stands in the Capitol rotunda.

• John Wesley Powell, who overcame the handicap of only one arm and battled the elements, mutiny, and starvation to explore the entire length of the Grand Canyon.

• Annie Sullivan, an orphaned and nearly blind pauper who grew up to work "miracles," teaching a determined Helen Keller—blind, deaf, and mute—to read, write, and speak. (They are buried here together.)

• Joe Louis, the boxing sharecropper's son who pounded Germany's Max Schmeling to the Yankee Stadium canvas in only two minutes, symbolically crushing the Nazi threat.

• Medgar Evers, a black civil rights worker in Mississippi whose depth of courage and conviction have rarely, if ever, been exceeded in American history.

• John F. Kennedy, who echoed some advice Americans will never forget: "Ask not what your country can do for you; ask what you can do for your country."

Recalling these lives touches many facets of our history, including the Revolutionary and Civil Wars, the only impeachment of a president, the early years of the women's movement, the Scopes "Monkey" Trial, both World Wars, the story of the FBI, and the growth of the U.S. space program. There are glimpses of American painting, sculpture, literature, science, and medicine. As a group the subjects' lives span more than two centuries, from George Washington to Omar Bradley and Joe Louis. In that time our country has grown from 13 struggling colonies to 50 United States casting their influence to every corner of the world.

The nation's growth was not achieved without cost. In a separate section we pay tribute to the Unknown Soldiers of six wars who are buried in Washington. Their life stories will never be known, yet their sacrifices make them as important as any person celebrated in this book. They represent more than a million men and women who have served and died for our country.

We have personally visited the graves of all the persons we write about, not only because a gravesite visit tends to give focus to what we know about a person but also because it often adds an insight. The tiny marker, for example, on the grave of Mathew Brady, a major figure in American photography, gives mute testimony to his impoverishment late in life. The mystery writer, Dashiell Hammett, was buried under a simple stone inscribed "Samuel D. Hammett," a final punctuation to his own mysterious life. John A. Joyce littered his headstone with examples of his poetry and philosophy, hoping to get a little postmortem recognition.

For readers who may want to see the headstones, we have included at the end of the book directions for locating each grave. Whether or not our book inspires readers to visit gravesites, we hope *Milestones Into Headstones* enlarges their Washington experience and that wherever it is read it may serve as a kind of catalog to our imagined museum of 50 Americans memorably involved in their own times and their nation's heritage.

The Adams Memorial. Credit: Peter Exton

Henry Adams

Historian, Man of Letters

b. February 16, 1838 Boston, Massachusetts
d. March 27, 1918 Washington, D.C.
Rock Creek

What should become of such a child of the seventeenth and eighteenth centuries, when he should wake up to find himself required to play the game of the twentieth?. . . As it happened, he never got to the point of playing the game at all; he lost himself in the study of it.

The Education of Henry Adams

When Henry Brooks Adams was a boy of six or seven, he had a loud argument with his mother. He hated school, he was never going again, and nothing she said could make him do otherwise. Just as his protests were reaching peak volume, the door to his grandfather's upstairs library opened. The old man, nearly 80, emerged and descended the stairs. He put on his hat, took the youngster firmly by the hand, and marched out the door. All without a word. Silently they walked toward the town, Henry too dumbfounded to try running away. Only after he had been placed at his school desk was young Adams released; and just as silently as they had come, his grandfather departed.

Perhaps it's not unique for grandfathers to help mothers with disobedient children. Not unique, that is, unless the grandfather is John Quincy Adams, sixth President of the United States.

Henry Adams was born into one of the most distinguished families in America. John Adams, our second President, was his great-grandfather; and Charles Francis Adams, his father, was Minister to Great Britain during the Civil War. It is no wonder that an Adams child would be led by the hand of his ancestry to write the history of the United States. Henry, with an ideal balance of intellect and sensitivity, was that child. He is still revered as one of the greatest historians produced by this country.

After graduating from Harvard in 1858, Henry spent a decade trying to figure out what to do with his life. He went to Europe with the general aim of learning German, but after two years filled mostly with travel, theater, riding and fencing lessons, he concluded shamefully that he had been "a mere tourist, and nothing else." On his return to the United States in 1860, he began an apprenticeship in the traditional Adams profession of politics by serving as personal secretary to his father, who had just been re-elected to Congress.

Early in 1861 Charles Francis Adams was sent to London as Lincoln's Minister to Great Britain, and Henry continued there as his secretary. Before leaving the United States, however, Henry secretly arranged with *The New York Times* to be the paper's anonymous London correspondent. Since he was a member of the U.S. delegation, which was forbidden "all communications with the press" during this sensitive time of war, accepting the position as reporter was a violation that if discovered could create serious repercussions for himself, his father, and British-American relations. For two years, Henry secretly wrote weekly dispatches for the *Times*, walking an uneasy tightrope between his two employers. When he came under attack for criticizing London society in an article written for another paper, Henry quit the *Times* for fear of being exposed. His father was never the wiser.

While in England, Henry began to dabble in history. Intrigued by the Captain John Smith-Pocahontas legend, he decided to investigate its truth by examining Smith's four accounts of his capture by Chief Powhatan and last-second rescue by the chief's beautiful daughter. The legend was firmly established as fact in Virginia, and Adams relished the thought that "Virginia aristocracy . . . will be utterly gravelled" if he could prove it false. After painstakingly comparing Smith's stories, he concluded that the legend was a fabrication. More inflammatory was his suggestion that Smith had concocted the whole thing to help himself gain public employment. Virginians, of course, were outraged when Adams's study was published in 1867. He was accused of attacking "the character of a celebrated woman," and was denounced as a Massachusetts upstart who cared little for the truth about two historical figures who had not come from "the barren soil of New England." Nonetheless, the young historian's study was well done and has never been successfully refuted.

By the time Henry had returned from England in 1868, he

had concluded that a life in government was not for him. He had no desire to "go down into the rough and tumble" of politics. Still an Adams, though, Henry could not abandon that arena altogether. He moved to Washington and set up shop as a political writer, urging solutions to many of the problems facing the postwar United States. Among those problems was President Grant, who may have been a brilliant military leader but whose startling ineptitude in the White House had ushered in a wave of boundless corruption. Try as he may to alert the public to Grant's incompetence, Adams found Americans unwilling to turn against the Civil War hero.

In 1870, Adams succumbed to pressure from friends and family and accepted a position as assistant professor of medieval history at Harvard, although he insisted that he knew very little about the subject. The college president replied, "If you will point out to me anyone who knows more, Mr. Adams, I will appoint him." Though Henry may not have been aware of his own talents, his feel for history was already apparent to others. During his seven years at Harvard, and a century after his country's birth, Adams began the school's first courses devoted solely to American history.

He also got married. Henry's bride was Marion Hooper, an intelligent, stimulating woman known to friends as Clover. Her family was well established in Massachusetts, meeting the approval of all the Adamses except Henry's brother Charles, who exclaimed, "By heavens! No! They're all crazy as coots. She'll kill herself just like her aunt." Despite rumors of mental instability in the Hooper clan, Henry and Clover were extremely happy together and could not have taken the remark seriously.

In 1877, the Adamses left Harvard and Boston for Washington, where Henry could research his first great project, the nine-volume *History of the United States*, completed in 1888. Built around the administrations of Thomas Jefferson and James Madison, the *History* has been called "the greatest historical work in English, with the possible exception of the *Decline and Fall*" [*of the Roman Empire* by Edward Gibbon]. When not absorbed in his research, Henry joined Clover in presiding over afternoon teas at their home on Lafayette Square. These teas were open only to those who met the Adamses' approval in mind and character, and included such as Henry James, John Hay, Oliver Wendell Holmes, Jr., Edith Wharton, John La Farge, Carl Schurz, Simon Newcomb, Clarence King, and William Dean Howells. Although they lived across the square in the White House, presidents were not guaranteed admittance.

A dark cloud descended on the Adams household when Mr. Hooper died in the spring of 1885. Clover had maintained an unusually close relationship with her father for many years, which at times seemed to rival her devotion to Henry. At his death she was unconsolable. She sank into an unremitting depression which ended with her suicide on December 6 of that year. Henry was crushed. He retreated into his work, severing social ties. Although he would live another 33 years, Henry would call it his "posthumous" existence.

A trip to Japan the year after her death gave Henry an inspiration for a monument to be placed over Clover's grave. Engaging the sculptor Augustus St. Gaudens, Henry vaguely suggested a figure in "calm reflection" that would blend elements of East and West. In the end it was the image of his apprentice, a blanket draped over his head, that became St. Gaudens's model. The resulting bronze figure, neither male nor female, has been hailed as the artist's finest work. Without an inscription of any kind, the memorial has invited countless interpretations over the years. Mark Twain saw all of human grief in the statue, perhaps reacting more to his friend's sorrow than to the art. Most people call the work "Grief," though St. Gaudens called it "The Peace of God." In later years, Eleanor Roosevelt frequently came for the comfort she found beneath the figure's "tranquil eyes."

For Henry, the anniversary of his wife's death would always be a difficult time, but although his mourning was extreme and perhaps exaggerated, he was not paralyzed by it. In 1889 he set out with his friend, the painter John La Farge, on a two year odyssey to the South Seas. In Samoa they witnessed the legendary Siva, a dazzling, sensual dance which missionaries were trying hard to suppress. Henry wrote to John Hay:

"You would rush for the next steamer if you could realize the beauty of some parts of the Siva. . . The pai-pai is a figure taboo by the missionaries . . . but it is still danced in the late hours of the night. Two or three women are the dancers, and they should be the best, especially in figure. They dance at first with the same movements, as far as I could see, that they use in many other figures. . . . Presently I noticed that the chief dancer's waistcloth seemed getting loose. This is their only dress, and it is nothing but a strip of cotton or tapa about eighteen inches wide, wrapped around the waist, with the end or corner tucked inside to hold it. Of course it constantly works loose, but the

natives are so well used to it that they always tighten it, and I never
yet have seen either man, woman or child let it fall by accident. In the
pai-pai, the women let their lava-lavas, as they are called, or siapas,
seem about to fall. The dancer pretends to tighten it, but only opens it
so as to show a little more thigh, and fastens it again so low as to
show a little more hip. Always turning about and moving with the chorus,
she repeats this process again and again, showing more legs and
hips every time, until the siapa barely hangs on her, and would fall
except that she holds it. At last it falls; she turns once or twice more,
in full view; then snatches up the siapa and runs away."

Although the Siva implied a great deal of "licentious" activity among the Samoans, Adams found the exact opposite to
be true. The dance was used to enhance a young woman's virtue, possibly increasing her marriage value "by the difference
of two or three fine mats and a dozen pigs." Reflecting on cultural differences, Adams noted, "Any European suddenly taken
to such a show would assume that the girl was licentious, and
if he were a Frenchman would probably ask for her. The chief
would be scandalised at European want of decency."

The 1890s saw Adams travel the globe almost continuously,
until in 1899 he found himself before the fabulous cathedral at
Chartres, outside Paris. His fascination with the Siva was only
a part of his growing reverence for womanhood; now he was
struck by the creativity unleashed by man's devotion to the Virgin Mary. In spite of God and Christ being male deities, the
European countryside was dotted with magnificent churches,
virtually all of them dedicated to Notre Dame, the Virgin. For
centuries, the faithful had placed their hopes, especially for
children, as much in her as in her Son. Henry spent dozens of
afternoons at Chartres contemplating the lives of those who had
created this cathedral to hold the tunic which Mary was believed to have worn at conception. The tunic and the *lava-lava*
may have been worlds apart, but they both symbolized virtuous
woman. As the new century dawned, Adams returned to America with the first draft of *Mont-St.-Michel and Chartres*, a
guidebook to the abbey and cathedral that encompassed far
more than sights. It recreated the 12th century for its readers.
Though the 20th century, the age of the "dynamo," had arrived, for Henry Adams, man's creativity had peaked in these
splendid 12th-century works inspired long ago "to please the
Queen of Heaven . . . to charm her till she smiled."

After dwelling on the harmony of the 12th century in *Mont-
St.-Michel and Chartres*, Henry turned his thoughts to his own

life and the baffling world of the 20th century. The result was his third-person autobiography, *The Education of Henry Adams*, which is widely praised as his crowning achievement. Having repeatedly attempted to educate himself in preparation for the new age, when the Virgin Mary would be replaced by the machine as mankind's idol, Henry concluded in the *Education* that he, and his countrymen, had failed to be ready. New information was coming too fast for anyone to understand its implications; trying to make order out of it was futile. A 20-year gap in the narrative, comprising his 13 years with Clover and the seven years following her death, hardly diminishes the power of the book. His descriptions of the period and his insights into a changing world are unexcelled.

In his last years, Henry Adams grew increasingly pessimistic about his country's future. He knew that a decline in morals would accompany technological progress. Although he called himself a man of 18th-century values forced to contend with the 20th, his life work still has meaning for modern Americans. In the words of one biographer, "Henry Adams offers to his fellow Americans the richest and most challenging image of what they are, what they have been, and what they may become."

Henry Adams Quoted

I tell you these are great times. Man has mounted science, and is now run away with. I firmly believe that before many centuries more, science will be the master of man. The engines he will have invented will be beyond his strength to control. Some day science may have the existence of mankind in its power, and the human race commit suicide by blowing up the world. Not only shall we be able to cruize(sic) in space, but I see no reason why some future generation shouldn't walk off like a beetle with the world on its back. . .

letter to brother Charles, 1862

The restoration of woman, which Christianity had begun, was principally effected in the twelfth century. . . As grace prevailed over the law, a great religious revolution took place. God if I may so speak, changed sex. The Virgin became the world's God, and took possession of almost all the temples and altars. Piety was converted into the enthusiasm of chivalrous gallantry. . .

Mont-St.-Michel and Chartres

God was Justice, Order, Unity, Perfection; He could not be human and imperfect, nor could the Son or the Holy Ghost be other than the Fa-

ther. The Mother alone was human, imperfect, and could love. . . If the Trinity was in its essence Unity, the Mother alone could represent whatever was not Unity; whatever was irregular, exceptional, outlawed; and this was the whole human race.

Mont-St.-Michel and Chartres

American history is so dull; there is not a woman in it.

remark

My country in 1900 is something totally different from my own country of 1860. I am wholly a stranger in it. Neither I, nor anyone else, understands it. The turning of a nebula into a star may somewhat resemble the change. All I can see is that it is one of compression, concentration, and consequent development of terrific energy, represented not by souls, but by coal and iron and steam.

letter to Charles Milnes Gaskell, 1900

He too serves a certain purpose who only stands and cheers.

The Education of Henry Adams

Friends are born, not made.

Education

Knowledge of human nature is the beginning and end of political education.

Education

Practical politics consists in ignoring facts.

Education

They know enough who know how to learn.

Education

I've watched people come into the White House and I've watched them go from the White House. Really what they do there doesn't matter a great deal.

remark

Suggested Reading:

The Education of Henry Adams
Ernest Samuels: *Henry Adams* (3 vols.)
David R. Contosta: *Henry Adams and the American Experiment*

Constance Bennett starred in over 50 films, often playing not-so-good girls, as in Outcast Lady. Credit: Library of Congress

Constance Bennett

Movie Actress

b. October 22, 1905 New York, New York
d. July 25, 1965 New York, New York
Arlington

The Depression was tough. At least for most
people. In 1932, one out of every four workers was jobless; the
country was grinding to a halt. But amid labor and manufactur-
ing problems, one industry survived and thrived—motion pictures. Americans seeking escape from the bleak times turned
to the dream-world of film and the glamorous stars of the 30s:
Clark Gable, Gary Cooper, Bette Davis, and the blonde, blue-
eyed Constance Bennett.

"My career as a movie star was virtually handed to me on a
silver platter," Constance Bennett once told an interviewer. The
sister of actress Joan Bennett and the daughter of silent film
director and matinee idol Richard Bennett, Constance came
from a family that had dominated the theater for five generations. Though her parents tried to steer her away from acting
by sending her to the best finishing schools in New York and
Paris, when she was still in her teens, her cool, willowy beauty
caught the eye of Samuel Goldwyn who insisted she try out for
a film he was producing. *Cytherea*, released in 1924, won no
awards, but Constance turned in a sparkling performance and
was launched on a career that included more than 50 films.

When sound arrived in the late 1920s, the movie world
turned upside down. Many of the stars of the silent films found
themselves out of work because of voices that were either too
shrill or too coarse. But for others, like Bennett, the cameras
continued to roll. In films like *Bed of Roses* (with Joel McCrea),
Affairs with Cellini (with Frederick March), and *After Office
Hours* (with Clark Gable), she established herself as a top box
office attraction.

In 1932, Bennett used her outspoken aggressiveness to land
a one-month, one picture contract with Warner Brothers for the
then unheard-of sum of $150,000. She reached the peak of her
fame as the sultry and sophisticated ghost in *Topper*, the com-

23

edy hit of 1937. Bennett and Cary Grant played a high-living couple who return to earth after being killed in a car accident and decide to help a henpecked bank president, Cosmo Topper, played by Leo G. Carroll. The sequel, *Topper Takes A Trip*, repeated the success the following year.

Bennett's private life was as sensational as her public life. Her volatile personality and love of conflict got her into numerous scrapes with the law that filled the Hollywood tabloids. She was once sued by a taxi company for failure to pay a fare of four dollars. "He took the long way around," she argued in her defense. But she lost. In another colorful case, she refused to pay an artist commissioned to paint her portrait. "That woman is an Amazon," Bennett declared when she saw the finished product. "I look like a sack of Portland cement with a rope tied in the middle." When the judge ruled in the artist's favor, Bennett responded by publicly kicking a hole in the canvas.

Bennett complemented her acting skills by being a successful businesswoman. Her broker claimed, "She's the shrewdest woman in the picture industry. I used to think Mary Pickford was, but she can't hold a candle to Constance. She knows the earning power and dividend record behind every bond and every share of stock she owns." At one point Bennett ran a cosmetics firm and lent her name to a designer's label. She kept her 5′ 4″, one-hundred-pound figure trim and was frequently on the list of the best-dressed women in Hollywood. Indeed, one gossip columnist reported that in 1941 Bennett spent a quarter million dollars on her wardrobe, a claim the actress hotly denied.

Husband-hopping also helped keep Bennett in the limelight. At 15 she eloped with a college student she met during the revelries of Easter weekend at the University of Virginia. At 19 she married millionaire playboy Philip Plant. In 1931, she paired up with the Marquis Henri de la Falaise de la Coudraye, the former husband of Gloria Swanson, one of Bennett's chief rivals in Hollywood. Ten years later she had a short, stormy marriage to film star Gilbert Roland. In 1946, she took her fifth and final husband, Colonel John Coulter, who had been in Hollywood as an advisor for Air Force training films.

Being an Air Force wife seemed to agree with Bennett. Although she never gave up her trademarks—her long, blonde hairdo, her matching gold barrette and cigarette holder—and occasionally went back to Hollywood to do a film, Bennett was happiest with her husband, living the nomadic military life. One of her favorite pastimes was playing poker, and she earned a reputation on the military bases for joining all-night games which she frequently won.

During the 1964 production of her last film, *Madame X*, with an all-star cast including Lana Turner, John Forsythe, Ricardo Montalban, and Burgess Meredith, Bennett commented on her years away from Hollywood: "Listen, there are worlds to enjoy that aren't made of mink and sables. And the world of mink and sables isn't free of drudgery and heartaches. It's all what you make it." In a career that spanned four decades, from silent films to talkies, and included a range of interests and activities, Constance Bennett made a lot of it.

Though late in life she still had her youthful good looks and had not added a pound to her figure, Bennett lied passionately about her age, even up to the end. Appropriately, the marker at Arlington Cemetery gives only her name and the date of her death. Movie stars, of course, never grow old.

Suggested Reading:

Joan Bennett and Lois Kibbee: *The Bennett Playbill*

The swaggering personas of Patton and Montgomery frame the rumpled figure of the GI General, Omar Bradley. Credit: U.S. Army

Omar Bradley

GI General

b. February 12, 1893 Clark, Missouri
d. April 8, 1981 New York, New York
Arlington

*Some of us will some day be bragging to our grandchildren that
'sure, General Bradley was a classmate of mine.'*

Cadet Dwight D. Eisenhower, 1915

It was April 1943, and Major General Omar
Bradley, the new commander of the II Corps in North Africa,
took the war correspondents by surprise. Unlike his prestige-
conscious predecessor George Patton, Bradley had decided to
brief the newsmen about upcoming operations in person, infor-
mally, and at their own headquarters. When he appeared, they
got another shock. Except for the stars on his helmet, Bradley
looked like any other GI in his canvas jacket, regulation pants,
and boots. He wore no ivory-handled pistol, no fancy buckles
or beret; he carried a map, not a riding crop. He was long and
lanky and spoke his few words with a quiet Missouri drawl.
From all appearances, this man seemed out of place and down-
right homely. At age 50, Bradley had never led a combat force
of any size and some of the correspondents were openly skep-
tical of his ability. They needn't have worried. Less than two
years later the briefing was remembered as the debut of America's "GI General," the man who let others take headlines for
flamboyance while he brilliantly led the largest American field
force in history across Europe to end World War II.

Affectionately called "Omie" by his wife and "Omer" by his
grandchildren, Omar Nelson Bradley was born in central Missouri and raised on rabbit and squirrel stew. His father died
just before his 15th birthday and Omar delivered papers and
worked as a section hand on the Wabash Railroad to help feed
the family. In 1911, having no money for college, he jumped at
the chance to go to West Point, where not only was the tuition
free, he actually got paid for going to school.

A war was raging in Europe when Cadet Bradley graduated in 1915, but he never got a chance to get in the fight. He was sent to teach military science at South Dakota State College while his contemporaries gained valuable battle experience. Later, he felt that the stateside duty had "washed out" his army career. For 20 years he was shuttled from one teaching assignment to another until he became assistant secretary to General George C. Marshall, the Army Chief of Staff, in 1939.

Bradley's relationship with Marshall changed his life. Impressed by his shrewd understanding of military tactics even though he had never been tested in combat, Marshall promoted Bradley from Lieutenant Colonel to Brigadier General and put him in charge of the Officer Candidate School at Fort Benning, Georgia. There, Bradley revolutionized the schooling of the "90-day wonders." Among other things, he insisted on rigorous physical training for the candidates, and for himself as well. Once, during a 25-mile night hike, some men groaned "Goddam the guy that organized this hike." Trudging along unrecognized, the 47-year-old Bradley chimed in "Yep, they ought to hang him."

With the outbreak of World War II, Marshall believed that Bradley could successfully apply his classroom skills to actual combat and sent him to join Eisenhower in North Africa. After taking over the II Corps, Bradley proved Marshall right as he teamed with Britain's Montgomery to drive the Axis forces off the continent. Next came Sicily, but just before the final routing of the enemy there Bradley was called to London to begin what Eisenhower called a "fancy new job." In only four months of combat experience, Bradley had convinced Marshall and Eisenhower that he was their best field commander. Now they wanted him to lead the American invasion of France on D-Day.

After months of planning, the Normandy assault was scheduled for June 6, 1944. On June 5, *Life* magazine speculated that since the unknown Bradley had "none of the theatrical qualities of a Patton or a Montgomery, his place in history will depend entirely on his performance. But if he does prove to be a great general, the kindness and simplicity which now make him a good man will make him a very great man." On the verge of greatness, Bradley mingled with troops preparing for the landing and reassured them that "we wouldn't be arranging this unless we were fairly sure it would work. I will see you on the beaches."

Bradley did see his men on the beaches, and his dust-covered jeep became a familiar sight along the front as the fighting stretched across France. In marked contrast to the prancing behavior of Patton and Montgomery, Bradley frequently put himself in danger, once chasing after a sniper who had almost killed him. By keeping the needs and difficulties of his GIs uppermost in his mind and by asking no special treatment for himself beyond what he gave them, Bradley became known as the "GI General." In his autobiography, *A Soldier's Story*, Bradley summed up his philosophy of military leadership:

. . . because war is as much a conflict of passion as it is of force, no commander can become a strategist until first he knows his men. . . For unless one values the lives of his soldiers and is tormented by their ordeals, he is unfit to command. He is unfit to appraise the cost of an objective in terms of human life.

. . . the well springs of humility lie in the field. For however arduous the task of a commander, he cannot face the men who shall live or die by his orders without sensing how much easier is his task than the one he has set them to perform.

Morale improved greatly when Bradley insisted on moving battlefield hospitals and first aid stations closer to the front to save more lives. It improved even more after the critically important port of Cherbourg had been taken, as Bradley arranged to have the huge booty of wine and champagne left by the Germans distributed equally among his troops.

In August 1944, Bradley assumed command of the newly formed 12th Army Group. At its peak, this force comprised 1.3 million men, thus making Bradley commander of the largest American field force ever. With Montgomery pushing from the north and Bradley advancing swiftly in the south, the Allies beat the Nazis back into Germany. On May 8, 1945, 11 months and two days after the landing at Normandy, Hitler's "thousand-year" Third Reich was done.

Having sent hundreds of thousands of soldiers into battle, Bradley took special pride in improving soldiers' medical care as head of the Veterans Administration after the war. In 1947 he succeeded Eisenhower as Army Chief of Staff, in 1949 he was made the first Chairman of the Joint Chiefs of Staff, and in 1951 he was promoted to the rank of General of the Army, becoming one of only five men to wear five stars.

Bradley presided over all U.S. Forces during the Korean War, which he called "the wrong war at the wrong place at the wrong time, and with the wrong enemy." When Douglas Mac-

Arthur, UN commander in Korea and another five-star general, flagrantly disobeyed President Truman's orders, Bradley concluded that the President "had every right to replace a general who defied his policy" and recommended that MacArthur be relieved.

In 1953 Bradley stepped down from active duty, although as a General of the Army he never formally retired. Thus, his career stretched from his entry into West Point in 1911 until he died in 1981, at 70 years the longest public service career in U.S. history.

Long after his 1915 prediction of an illustrious career for classmate Omar Bradley, Dwight Eisenhower wrote: "Bradley was the master tactician of our forces and in my opinion will eventually come to be recognized as America's foremost battle leader."

Suggested Reading:

Omar N. Bradley and Clay Blair: *A General's Life*

Mathew Brady

Photographer

b. 1823? Warren County, New York
d. January 15, 1896 New York, New York
Congressional

In the spring of 1861, Mathew Brady was on
top of the world. Internationally famous, rich, fashionable,
Brady had taken the fledgling craft of photography and ele-
vated it to art, attracting the most prominent Americans of his
time before his camera. He had established galleries in both
New York and Washington. And now, he committed his resources to recording a photographic history of the Civil War, a
project that would surely extend his fame and guarantee a bal-
looning of his wealth. But something went wrong. Expenses
and frustrated cameramen derailed his dream. In a few short
years Brady's money had evaporated, his employees had deserted, and his fame had become an irretrievable thing of the
past. The most significant figure in early American photography, Mathew Brady had gambled everything and lost.

Brady was born to a poor Irish family in the eastern Adiron-
dack Mountains in either 1823 or 1824—no record of his birth
exists. Around 1840 he came to New York, where he learned
to make daguerreotypes from Samuel F. B. Morse, the inventor
of the telegraph. With the eye of an artist and an en-
trepreneurial flair, the young photographer opened his first gallery to immediate success in 1844.

Not long after he had gone into business, Brady realized the
commercial potential in making portraits of famous personalities, and in 1851 published his *Gallery of Illustrious Americans*. Welcomed with much fanfare and critical acclaim, the
book of famous-name photographs made "Brady of Broadway" a
national figure. Photographing the famous became his trademark, typified by his presidential portraits spanning half a
century. Seeking out his illustrious subjects, posing them for
the camera and often asking no payment, Brady amassed a remarkable collection that included Abraham Lincoln, Ulysses S.
Grant, Daniel Webster, Walt Whitman, Mark Twain, Kit Car-

Bitter fighting took place on this field at Gettysburg, but Mathew Brady's record of the event seems more concerned with capturing his reflected image. Credit: Library of Congress

son, George Armstrong Custer, John J. Audubon, P. T. Barnum, and Tom Thumb. Selling small versions of these portraits was a mainstay of his business.

In its early years, photography wasn't considered much of an art; the palette and brush still reigned as the preferred way to have one's image preserved. Brady promoted that notion, often using his photographs as something of an outline (he used the term "auxiliary"), like tracing the lines of a slide projected on a sheet of paper. The photograph taken, touch-up artists then added color and highlights, eliminated blemishes and wrinkles, and sometimes worked over a portrait so thoroughly that the original photograph was almost completely obscured. But this was accepted practice, and a customer was certainly honored to have Brady himself do the brushwork. Thus, the label "Photo by Brady," which was stamped on every piece produced by his studio, could mean anything from an untouched print of a little child to an elaborately "improved" portrait of a national hero.

In 1858, Brady installed Alexander Gardner, an expert in

the wet-plate photographic process, as manager of his new Washington, D.C. gallery. Gardner was very gifted, both as a photographer and a businessman. While he initially proved a valuable asset to Brady's pursuits, establishing a gallery where Brady had earlier failed to do so, he eventually asserted the right of those directly involved in creating photographs to be recognized for their work, a change that Brady's lust for personal fame could not concede.

When the Civil War finally broke out, Brady hired teams of photographers to record it. These unheralded artists overcame severe hardships to cover virtually every important turn of the war, making more than 3,500 photographs. Brady himself spent most of the war in the comfortable surroundings of his New York studio, and when he did appear in the field there is no evidence that he operated a camera (by this time, his nearsightedness probably made focusing a camera impossible). Customarily, he designed the photograph to be taken and then stepped into the scene before the exposure was made. In this manner, Brady may have become the single most photographed individual in his own Civil War record. By war's end, Brady's idea of what photographs he could credit to himself extended to anything he could get his hands on.

The war project was a costly obsession with Brady, exhausting his personal fortune of $100,000. He ignored bills and the more profitable parts of his business to pursue it. Frustrated by unpaid wages and uncredited work, Brady's best photographers quit, many to join Gardner, who after 1862 had established his own gallery. Debtors plagued Brady until long after the war, when in 1875 the government finally purchased 2,000 of the war photographs for $25,000. But that only cleared his debts; financially, he never recovered.

Denied the recognition he felt he deserved, Brady spent most of his last years in Washington, D.C., falling further and further out of touch with advances in photography while continually pleading with the government to publish his war photographs. He had sacrificed everything to produce a collection of historic scenes, and never could accept that his effort would go unrewarded. Hobbled by a collison with a horse-carriage, nearly blind and penniless, Brady died in New York while attempting to arrange an exhibition of the war views.

Suggested Reading:

Dorothy Meserve Kunhardt and Philip B. Kunhardt, Jr.: *Mathew Brady and His World*

Wernher von Braun

Space Pioneer

b. March 23, 1912 Wirsitz, Germany (now Wyrzysk, Poland)
d. June 16, 1977 Alexandria, Virginia
Ivy Hill

It's hard to believe that less than 50 years ago space travel was no more than a fantasy to most people. For Wernher von Braun, however, it was a vision—a reality that would come in time. With a lifelong determination, von Braun pursued the dream of landing a human on another planet until on July 20, 1969, astronaut Neil Armstrong stepped onto the moon with the words "One small step for a man, a giant leap for mankind." Von Braun's contribution to that giant leap was considerable: he pioneered the first practical space rockets, orbited the first U.S. satellite, and harnessed the power—180 million horses worth—necessary to propel the Apollo crews to the moon.

Baroness Emmy von Braun, who knew her way around the universe with a telescope, gets the credit for developing her son's early interest in space. But she can be absolved of any blame for Wernher's spectacular childhood experiments. Once, he lashed fireworks rockets to a little wagon and went careening madly through the streets of Berlin, trailing a roar of fire and smoke. In other instances, his homemade rockets plunged into a fruit stand and a bakery. In love with rockets but bored with the classroom, von Braun failed math and physics in high school. But when he discovered that he needed to understand those subjects to pursue the possibility of space flight, he delved into them with a new perspective and wound up tutoring other students in courses he had failed only a short time before.

In 1930, von Braun joined the Society for Space Travel in Berlin. Although only a club of rocket enthusiasts, the Society counted many leading scientists among its members and von Braun, at 18, found himself at the forefront of rocket research. He then studied at the Institute of Technology in Zürich, Switzerland, where he experimented with the effects of space flight on mice. A rocket speeding away from the earth's surface would create a force many times that of gravity on a mouse—

or a human. To create the same force centrifugally for his experiments, von Braun fixed a belt-driven bicycle wheel horizontally on a table in his apartment. A mouse was placed in a container on the rim of the wheel, the wheel was set spinning until a force equivalent to that produced by a space-bound rocket had been achieved, and then the mouse was dissected to analyze the effects. Although von Braun learned a great deal from these experiments, his landlady didn't appreciate the mouse blood that ringed the walls of his room, and ordered him to move out.

In the early 1930s, von Braun's research came under the wing of the German army, which was intrigued by the possible use of rockets as weapons. In 1937, the 25-year-old von Braun was made technical director of a new research center in Peenemünde on the Baltic coast. By the outbreak of World War II, the Peenemünde team had successfully launched a number of rocket designs and was close to producing a guided rocket that could carry a one-ton military payload. Thirty-six hundred of the improved version of this rocket, named "Vergeltungswaffe Zwei" ("revenge weapon two"), or "V-2", by Nazi propaganda minister Goebbels, rained on London and Antwerp during the last year of the war. Never a supporter of the lethal use of his rockets, von Braun was jailed briefly by the Gestapo in 1944, charged with thinking too much about space travel and complaining about pressures to produce rocket weaponry. Only when the Nazis realized that rocket development would be lost without him was von Braun released.

At the end of World War II von Braun and 117 members of his research team, who chose to surrender to the Americans rather than the Soviets, were secretly taken to Fort Bliss, Texas. There they continued work on the V-2, imparted their knowledge to American scientists, and generally advanced the U.S. space program by leaps and bounds. Von Braun conducted numerous experiments in space and developed the Redstone rocket, which played an important role in America's early space program. In 1950, he was put in charge of the missile research center at Huntsville, Alabama, and in 1955 he became a U.S. citizen.

During the 1950s, the Russians made swift progress in their space program. Von Braun tried in vain to get U.S. officials to recognize the Soviet advances and to give him permission to orbit a satellite. Not until the Russians orbited Sputnik 1 in 1957 did they finally listen. Less than three months later von

Braun sent Explorer 1, the free world's first satellite, into orbit. Explorer 1 was followed by a steady succession of launches carrying increasingly heavier payloads, including manned space capsules. Von Braun's responsibility was to build rockets that could push the heavier weights into orbit—and beyond. His efforts culminated in the Saturn V booster rocket that sent the first space craft to the moon in 1968. Von Braun's earliest rockets had a thrust of a few hundred pounds; the Saturn V engines hit the launch pad with an incredible thrust of 7.6 million pounds—equivalent to twice the power that could be generated if every river in North America were dammed.

Von Braun's successes stemmed not only from his own knowledge and creativity, but also from his ability to lead a diverse team of scientists and engineers. He had directed one of the world's earliest rocket research groups when he was only 22, and had long understood the importance of teamwork to the challenges of space technology. Although immersed in sophisticated scientific research, von Braun could surface to describe his work in simple terms to the uninitiated, as when he told some congressmen about one of his satellites: "For miles to the gallon it puts a Volkswagen to shame." On the other hand, his enthusiasm for reaching into the heavens led him to make occasional statements that were hard to believe. In his novel *The Mars Project*, which detailed a complex mission to Mars based on available scientific knowledge, von Braun claimed that "the logistics requirements for a large, elaborate expedition to Mars are no greater than those for a minor military operation extending over a limited theatre of war."

A scientist of the highest caliber, von Braun was by no means a sallow-skinned egghead. An avid outdoorsman, he stalked reindeer in Norway and bear, moose, and caribou on the Alaskan tundra. He was an expert glider pilot and an experienced sailor and fisherman. But none of these outside activities was as dear to him as his first love—space. Not long before he died of cancer in 1977, von Braun told a friend: "Can you name me many guys who have had the great good fortune to spend practically all their lives in responsible positions to help their boyhood dreams come true? If I have to go tomorrow, I can look back at a full, exciting and deeply rewarding life. What else can a man ask for?"

Suggested Reading:
Erik Bergaust: *Wernher von Braun*
Heather M. David: *Wernher von Braun*

The *"Michelangelo of the Capitol," Constantino Brumidi.*
Credit: Architect of the Capitol

Constantino Brumidi

Painter

b. July 26, 1805 Rome, Italy
d. February 18, 1880 Washington, D.C.
Glenwood

I have no longer any desire for fame or fortune. My one ambition and my daily prayer is that I may live long enough to make beautiful the Capitol of the one country on earth in which there is liberty.

These were the words of a poor Italian artist, revolutionary, and political refugee, Constantino Brumidi. Although a nearly fatal accident prevented Brumidi from fully realizing his dream, during 26 years he covered the walls and ceilings of the seat of the United States government with such an impressive array of frescoes and murals that soon after his death he was hailed as the "Michelangelo of the Capitol." Indeed, if any one man can be said to be responsible for the artistic magnificence of the interior of the Capitol, that man is Constantino Brumidi. His work set the tone and standard for all subsequent decoration.

Born in Italy to a Greek father and an Italian mother, Brumidi showed great talent for drawing as a boy and entered the Rome Academy of Fine Arts. During the pontificate of Pius IX he was awarded a gold medal for a portrait of the pope and helped restore the Raphael frescoes in the Vatican.

Despite his close ties to the Catholic church, Brumidi was opposed to papal rule in Rome and in 1848 he joined a popular rebellion which forced the pope to flee the city. When Pius IX returned with the aid of French troops, Brumidi was thrown into jail for 14 months and then released on condition that he leave the country. Like many other political refugees—then and now—he chose America as his haven. On September 18, 1852, almost 50 years old and speaking little English, Constantino Brumidi landed in New York.

After two years of decorating churches, Brumidi conceived a plan for covering the interior of the United States Capitol with frescoes. Since the artist had no samples of his work, it was suggested he demonstrate his skill by decorating the room used by the Committee on Agriculture with suitable paintings. Completed in 1855, these frescoes, made by applying color to wet plaster, are some of the first true frescoes undertaken in this country.

Congressional reaction to Brumidi's work was mixed. For his subject, the artist had chosen a combination of Classical scenes and events from American history. One politician complained "there are too many gods and goddesses and not a single specimen of cattle, horses, sheep, maize, grain or corn which are now found in this country." Others praised the frescoes' "distinguished worth," and they were popular enough for Brumidi to be put on the payroll as chief artist of the Capitol at a salary of eight dollars a day.

With his European training, Brumidi was most familiar with Classical and Renaissance motifs and initially these dominated his painting. As his work continued, however, and as he learned the dramatic history of his adopted country, he turned increasingly for inspiration to the American past and the Revolution. Slowly, over the years, the Capitol became a kind of picture book visually recounting the stirring story of America.

Although little is known of Brumidi's personal life, the pride he took in his new nationality can be seen in his signature on the second work he completed for the government, a mural depicting George Washington at Yorktown. Brumidi responded to disgruntled artists who complained of the foreign influence in his work by signing this piece conspicuously, "C. Brumidi, Artist, Citizen of the U.S." The truth is, native painters were probably jealous of Brumidi's ability; few, if any, American-born artists were trained in fresco painting or had experience painting on such a large scale.

Brumidi's decoration in the President's Room is often considered his best work. These paintings took five years to complete and include five ceiling-to-floor panels, each containing an elegant portrait of a member of Washington's first Cabinet. Here Brumidi created a *trompe-l'oeil* effect by painting right on the wall what appear to be ornately carved frames for the portraits. Although most of the surfaces the artist covered are flat, by realistically depicting niches, moldings, columns, and sculptured figures, he added a third dimension to the walls of the building.

Brumidi's most important and most difficult work was the

huge fresco in the dome of the rotunda. He chose for his subject "The Apotheosis of Washington." Working on a wooden scaffolding 180 feet above the floor, Brumidi completed the piece in 11 months. The painting is a combination of mythological and historical figures showing George Washington seated at the center on a rainbow and clouds, surrounded by 13 females representing the original states. The woman representing Freedom, directly below Washington in the dome, is said to be a portrait of Lola Germon, a beautiful 18-year-old actress who became Brumidi's wife about 1860.

In 1877, Brumidi began his final work, a fresco in grey, imitating a sculptural frieze ringing the base of the dome and depicting the early history of America. For this, the 72-year-old artist rigged a special sliding scaffold. Every morning at 10:00 A.M., the striking figure with snow-white hair and beard was hoisted by a system of pulleys to what he called his "shop." His descent in the afternoon was an event of the day for visitors who watched anxiously until Brumidi landed. On October 1, 1879, Brumidi's painting chair tipped over, leaving him dangling from the rung of a ladder 60 feet above the ground. After 15 minutes, help finally reached him, but the fright and shock were so great that he never returned to his work. Five months later Brumidi died quietly at his home on G Street.

Suggested Reading:

Myrtle Cheney Murdock: *Constantino Brumidi, Michelangelo of the United States Capitol*

William Jennings Bryan stirs 'em up during the presidential campaign of 1908. Credit: Library of Congress

William Jennings Bryan

Political Leader, Orator

> b. March 19, 1860 Salem, Illinois
> d. July 26, 1925 Dayton, Tennessee
> Arlington

I might as well put up a trapeze on my front lawn and compete with some professional athlete as go out speaking against Bryan.

William McKinley

In 1800, 95 percent of the U.S. population lived on farms. Most of our founding fathers, including Washington and Jefferson, were farmers. Today, the nation's farm population has dwindled to less than 3 percent and most of us pursue life, liberty, and happiness in cities. If there is a turning point in our history when the principal occupation of early America yielded to urban growth, it is the presidential election of 1896. If anyone personifies the farmer's resistance to that change, it is the man who lost the election, William Jennings Bryan.

While industry was drastically reshaping America's eastern and northern cities during the 1880s, William Jennings Bryan was practicing law near the waves of grain surrounding Lincoln, Nebraska. The heartland values of honest, hard work and a literally-read Bible were deeply impressed on his thinking. With governmental attention shifting to big business, Nebraska farmers saw in Bryan an able voice for their needs and elected him to Congress in 1890.

After two terms in Congress, Bryan was defeated in a bid for the Senate in 1894. Undaunted, he aimed higher the next time around, setting his sights on the White House in 1896. A little-known ex-congressman from the midwest, Bryan was ignored by senior members of the Democratic party. A poll just prior to the convention rated him a distant seventh in the race for the nomination; experts didn't give him a chance. But a chance was all he needed, and he got it when he was asked to close a portion of the platform debate.

43

Bryan was a spellbinding orator with a talent for sensing the mood and desires of the common man. Although he was asked to address a complex economic issue, it was not his way to allow it to remain so. His discussion of bimetallism versus a gold standard was transformed into a polemic on good and evil— those who favored a gold standard were corrupt, immoral city dwellers out to destroy the country's backbone of moral, hardworking farmers and laborers. "Burn down your cities and leave our farms," he said, "and your cities will spring up again as if by magic; but destroy our farms and the grass will grow in the streets of every city in the country!" The delegates thundered their approval. As he spoke, Bryan was in complete control, his booming voice carrying to the most distant listener, the pauses hushed with anticipation. The speech ended in a dramatic climax when Bryan equated gold advocates with the likes of Pontius Pilate:

If they dare to come out into the open field and defend the gold standard as a good thing, we will fight them to the uttermost. Having behind us the producing masses of this nation and the world, supported by the commercial interests, the laboring interests, and the toilers everywhere, we will answer their demand for a gold standard by saying to them: 'You shall not press down upon the brow of labor this crown of thorns. You shall not crucify mankind upon a cross of gold!'

Hysteria followed, and the next day Bryan was nominated for president at the age of 36.

Bryan had gone into the convention a harmless long shot, but came out a very serious contender for the presidency. He had focused the discontent of millions of rural Americans creating a panic among the supporters of his opponent, William McKinley. McKinley's men turned to the industrial fat cats with predictions of economic chaos should Bryan be elected. The response was huge contributions to the McKinley campaign and open threats of dismissal for employees who dared to vote for Bryan. In the first big money campaign in our history, McKinley outspent Bryan nearly 25 to one.

Bryan knew that his oratory was his greatest strength and that his votes were in the agricultural west and south. Breaking an old tradition against presidential candidates personally stumping for votes, he traveled an unheard-of 18,000 miles in a wild whistle-stop campaign, making more than six hundred speeches before over five million people. But it was not enough against the unified powers of industry, banks, insurance, oil, and most of the press. McKinley won by a narrow 4 percent of the popular vote. His election signaled the arrival of the industrial 20th century and marked the ebb of the farmer's strength in national politics.

Bryan continued to represent the common man, but as a reflection of the decline in rural influence, he lost two more presidential elections (1900, 1908) by progressively wider margins. Called the "Great Commoner," Bryan was seen by many as a naive and simpleminded example of the people for whom he spoke. Yet he was an effective politican who ranked as a leader in the Democratic party for almost 30 years. And in spite of his adherence to values of a passing era, Bryan was very progressive in much of his thinking. He advocated women's suffrage, curbs on trade monopolies, a federal income tax, and an eight-hour day long before those ideas became law.

At the Democratic convention of 1912, the nomination of Woodrow Wilson was due in large part to the efforts of Bryan. After Wilson's election, Bryan was made Secretary of State as a reward for his support. Through that office, he hoped to become an international peacemaker, and to that end, succeeded in negotiating "treaties of investigation" with 30 nations. These treaties stipulated enforced "cooling off" periods in any dispute, allowing time for a commission to investigate the situation. However, Bryan's peace-no-matter-what policies led to his resignation in 1915, when he opposed Wilson's denunciation of the German sinking of the *Lusitania.*

Amid the turmoil leading to our involvement in World War I, the temperance movement was also gathering steam. As an upstanding, righteous advocate of prohibition, Bryan insisted on serving grape juice at official functions, a very unpopular move in Washington's diplomatic circles. Dubbed "grape-juice diplomacy," this habit was not missed when Bryan left office.

Bryan devoted his last ten years to preaching the fundamentalist gospel and denouncing the "menace of Darwinism." His crusade against the concept of human evolution from apes took him from pulpit to pulpit around the country, but in the summer of 1925 he was made to defend his beliefs from the witness stand in the famous Scopes "Monkey" Trial.

John T. Scopes was a high school biology teacher in Dayton, Tennessee, who was being tried for breaking a state law prohibiting the teaching of evolution theory in public schools. Bryan had helped put the law on Tennessee's books and was invited to join in prosecuting the case. His defense counterpart was Clarence Darrow, the wily criminal lawyer.

There was not much question about Scopes's guilt—he <u>had</u> broken the law. But Bryan and Darrow were like two salivating dogs eager to tear into one another over the bone of Darwinism. After several days of preliminary sparring, Bryan was called upon to testify. Always confident of his cause, he jumped at the challenge and took the stand. For the next two hours Darrow picked apart Bryan's beliefs, confounding him with questions that led him into contradictory traps. He could only match Darrow's prepared examination with retreats into scripture, and in the end he had suffered a staggering humiliation. Bryan vowed revenge in his closing argument, but Darrow deprived him of the opportunity when he exercised his option to forego closing arguments. (Darrow had supported Bryan in politics and maintained a healthy respect for the power of his oratory.)

The sweltering mid-summer heat and the assault on his religion evidently took its toll on the 65-year-old Bryan. He died five days after the trial ended, while revising for publication the rebuttal he was unable to deliver in Dayton.

The Great Commoner Speaks Out

When God made man he gave him a soul and warned him that in the next world he would be held accountable for the deeds done in the flesh; but when man created the corporation he could not endow that corporation with a soul, so that if it escapes punishment here it need not fear the hereafter. . . We must assume that man in creating the corporation had in view the welfare of society, and the people who create must retain the power to restrict and to control. . . We can never become so enthusiastic over the corporation . . . as to forget the God-made man.

Speech before Chicago Association of Commerce, 1896

Did you ever raise a radish? You put a small black seed into the black soil and in a little while you return to the garden and find the full-grown radish. . . What mysterious power reaches out and gathers from the ground the particles which give it form and size and flavor? Whose is the invisible brush that transfers to the root, growing in darkness, the hues of the summer sunset? If we were to refuse to eat anything until we could understand the mystery of its creation we would die of starvation—but mystery, it seems, never bothers us in the dining room; it is only in the Church that it causes us to hesitate.

"The Value of An Ideal" (lecture)

Below are some excerpts from Bryan's undelivered, 13,000-word rebuttal to Darrow and the evolutionists:

Religion is not hostile to learning; Christianity has been the greatest patron learning has ever had. But Christians know that 'the fear of the Lord is the beginning of wisdom' now just as it has been in the past, and they therefore oppose the teaching of guesses that encourage godlessness among the students.

. . . Some of the more rash advocates of evolution are wont to say that evolution is as firmly established as the law of gravitation or the Copernican theory. The absurdity of such a claim is apparent when we remember that anyone can prove the law of gravitation by throwing a weight in the air, and that anyone can prove the roundness of the earth by going around it, while no one can prove evolution to be true in any way whatever.

. . . The evolutionist does not undertake to tell us how protozoa, moved by interior and resident forces, sent life up through the various species, and cannot prove that there was actually any such compelling power at all. And yet, the school children are asked to accept their guesses. . .

. . . Darwin attempts to trace the mind of man back to the mind of lower animals . . . he endeavors to trace man's moral nature back to the animals. It is all animal, animal, animal, with never a thought of God or of religion.

When Darwin entered upon his scientific career he was 'quite orthodox and quoted the Bible as an unanswerable authority'. . . It was after [he wrote The Origin of Species] *that 'very gradually, with many fluctuations', his belief in God became weaker. He traces this decline for us and concludes by telling us that he cannot pretend to throw the least light on . . . religious problems. . . Then comes the flat statement that he 'must be content to remain an Agnostic'; and to make clear what he means by the word, agnostic, he says that 'the mystery of the beginning of all things is insoluble by us'—not by him alone, but by everybody. Here we have the effect of evolution upon its most distinguished exponent; it led from an orthodox Christian, believing every word of the Bible and in a personal God, down and down and down to helpless and hopeless agnosticism.*

. . . How can any teacher tell his students that evolution <u>does not tend</u> to destroy his religious faith? How can an honest teacher <u>conceal</u> from his students the effect of evolution upon Darwin himself?

. . . The law has not heretofore required the writing of the word 'poison' on poisonous doctrines. The bodies of our people are so valuable that druggists and physicians must be careful to properly label all poisons; why not be as careful to protect the spiritual life of our people from the poisons that kill the soul?

. . . The world needs a Saviour more than it ever did before. . .

Suggested Reading:

Louis W. Koenig: *Bryan: A Political Biography of William Jennings Bryan*

Lawrence W. Levine: *Defender of the Faith—William Jennings Bryan: the Last Decade*

William Jennings Bryan: *The Memoirs of William Jennings Bryan*

Richard E. Byrd

Aviator, Explorer

b. October 25, 1888 Winchester, Virginia
d. March 11, 1957 Boston, Massachusetts
Arlington

June 1, 1934:
I awakened with a violent start, as if I had been thrown down a well
in my sleep. I found myself staring wildly into the darkness of the
shack, not knowing where I was. The weakness that filled my body
when I turned in the sleeping bag and tried to throw the flashlight on
my wristwatch was an eloquent reminder. I was Richard E. Byrd,
temporarily sojourning at Latitude 80° 08' South, and not worth a
damn to myself or anybody else.

Richard E. Byrd, aviator, explorer, adventurer;
alone in a tiny outpost at the bottom of the world. Byrd went
there to study weather conditions in the interior of Antarctica,
but the real story of his stay is not meteorological. Because of
carbon monoxide fumes leaking from his stove, Byrd's solo became a nightmare from which he barely escaped. The real
story is how Byrd survived four months of insidious poisoning.
Why would anyone volunteer for a hazardous, solitary post
miles from help? Byrd wasn't just anyone.

A native of Winchester, Virginia, Byrd was reared in the
open country of the Shenandoah Valley. At 12, he accepted an
invitation from a family friend in Manila and boarded a train
for San Francisco, the first stop on a trip which would eventually take him around the world. Byrd spent nearly a year in
the Philippines and returned home only when a cholera epidemic threatened his life. When his tramp steamer docked in
Boston, Byrd had no doubt about the future: he would be an
adventurer.

World War I brought him the chance he hoped for. In 1916,
after graduating from the Naval Academy, the slender, quiet
lieutenant arrived in Pensacola, Florida, for training as a naval
aviator. The crash rate was high at Pensacola but Byrd was

Richard Byrd, cooking on the stove that nearly killed him.
Credit: National Archives

fearless, flying solo after only six hours of instruction. He realized immediately that aviation would change the world and vowed to be a part of that change.

In 1926, Byrd mounted the first airborne expedition to the North Pole. Using Spitzbergen, Norway, as a base, Byrd and his copilot, Floyd Bennett, took off on May 9 for their 1500-mile flight. Nearing their destination, Byrd was dismayed to see the starboard engine leaking oil. He quickly calculated the chances of successfully landing on the ice and repairing the engine, and decided to continue. His faith in the plane was justified: like a minor wound, the leak healed itself and soon they were over the Pole. When they returned to the United States, Byrd and Bennett were celebrated as heros and awarded the Congressional Medal of Honor by President Coolidge.

Following his northern success, the restless aviator turned his attention to the Antarctic, one of the last unexplored regions of the world. "It is now my ambition," he wrote, "not only to take an aircraft to the loneliest continent—Antarctica; but to take it to the loneliest part of that continent—the Pole."

On November 29, 1929, one month after the bottom fell out of the stock market, Byrd took off from his base camp—christened Little America—and made the first flight to the South Pole. When news of his triumph reached the United States, the wry comment came back that the best place to be was with Byrd at the Pole; at least there one didn't have to worry about the stock market crash. Despite the financial crisis, there were celebrations and awards, including promotion to Rear Admiral, for the conquering hero. Byrd had become one of the most famous explorers of the century.

With these experiences behind him, Byrd organized a new expedition in 1934 to photograph and map Antarctica by air, and carry out scientific research. Though not as newsworthy as his first two polar exploits, this expedition proved to be the most controversial. One of the projects was to man a weather station 125 miles in the interior of the continent. Byrd had originally planned to send three men to the base, but as preparations neared completion, he decided to go alone. He wanted the solitude, he said, and time to think.

On March 22, Byrd arrived at the 9' × 13' shack which would be his home for the next seven months. He had plenty of food, and for heat there was an old caboose stove which had been converted to oil. The first few weeks passed uneventfully, with outside temperatures hovering at a cool −50°F. "Cold does queer things," Byrd noted in his journal, "below −60°F if there is the slightest breeze, you can hear your breath freeze as it floats away, making a sound like Chinese firecrackers." At times he waxed poetic at the coming winter night: "The sun rose this morning around 9:30 but never really left the horizon. Huge and red and solemn, it rolled like a wheel along the edge for about two and a half hours when the sunrise met the sunset at noon." Turning to more immediate concerns, on April 8 he wrote prophetically, "I'm rather worried about a blockage in the pipe; unless the fumes from the stove escape to the surface, I shall have trouble." Byrd made several attempts to fix the stove, but by early May his aching eyes and head were clear symptoms of carbon monoxide poisoning. Byrd's hut had become a prison and he was slowly, painfully dying. Although he refused to mention it in his radio reports to Little America, Byrd's increasingly garbled transmissions alerted the base camp that something was wrong. When Byrd ducked direct questions about his condition, a rescue mission was mounted. At midnight on August 10, the snow tractor arrived. Byrd was still alive, but barely. His eyes were wild and sunken, his face scabby, and his hair long and disheveled. The hut was filthy, littered with empty cans Byrd was too weak to throw out. It was two months before he was well enough to return to Little America. Later, he described his departure from the weather station:

I climbed the hatch and never looked back. Part of me remained forever at Latitude 80° 08' South: what survived of my youth, my vanity, perhaps, and certainly my skepticism. On the other hand, I did take away something that I had not fully possessed before: appreciation of the sheer beauty of being alive, and a set of humble values. . . A man doesn't begin to attain wisdom until he recognizes that he is no longer indispensable.

Byrd returned to the United States a changed man. His solitary vigil had scarred him both physically and mentally. Although the Navy gave him command of two more Antarctic expeditions, it neatly avoided handing him any real responsibility. Publicly he was praised, the first man to fly to both Poles, but officially there were questions: Why did Byrd risk his entire expedition by moving alone to the station? Why didn't he radio for help when he needed it? What really happened? The answer may rest with his private papers, which have not yet been released by his family. Richard E. Byrd was a complex man whose great reserve gave the impression of a deep and mysterious personality. When he died in 1957, the world mourned the passing of one of the last great explorers, a man who accomplished and experienced much, and bore it all with grace and dignity.

Suggested Reading:

Edwin P. Hoyt: *The Last Explorer*
Richard E. Byrd: *Alone*

John Clem

Drummer Boy of Chickamauga

b. August 13, 1851 Newark, Ohio
d. May 13, 1937 San Antonio, Texas
Arlington

He was a determined little sprout. The war to preserve the Union was on, and all 3½ feet and 40 pounds of John Clem had decided that his help was "obviously needed." Immune to such comments as "We can't use infants here," the eager nine-year-old simply attached himself to the 23rd Michigan Regiment as a drummer boy and pitched in to win the war. Before long, Clem had become famous for his pluck and tenacity in battle, earning several popular nicknames, among them "Johnny Shiloh" and the "Drummer Boy of Chickamauga." He was also celebrated as the youngest recruit to take up arms in the Civil War, and finally gave up soldiering only after President Woodrow Wilson refused to let him go along with the American forces being sent to Europe in World War I.

Like Grant, Sherman, Sheridan, and Stanton, young Johnny Clem was a buckeye from Ohio. A few weeks after Southern guns had opened up on Fort Sumter, his mother was run over by a train and killed; a fortnight later he left home intent on joining the Union army. Undaunted by rejections of his offer to help save the Union, Clem stowed himself away on a troop train bound for Cincinnati. He eluded his father's attempts to bring him home, and with a little perseverance succeeded in getting himself accepted into the 23rd Michigan.

More or less adopted by the regiment (he wouldn't go away), Clem was given a drum, a musket with a sawed-off barrel to fit his size, and a cut-down uniform that left him plenty of room for growth. Since he wasn't technically allowed to be mustered into the ranks, the regiment's officers chipped in to pay him a private's wages of $13 a month, and he drew the same rations as everyone else. At night he shared a tent with two full size soldiers.

Clem wasn't much help as a drummer. He could only beat out the command for "advance"—"retreat" wasn't in his repertoire. So perhaps serendipity played a part in making his fame when at the Battle of Shiloh a hunk of shrapnel demolished his little drum, knocking him down. Bravely he picked himself up and started firing his abbreviated weapon at the enemy. Although other soldiers at Shiloh were bigger and older, few had ever seen any actual combat, and the sight of this near-babe courageously battling the rebels inspired everyone around him. After the raw Union troops had managed to drive off the Confederates on the battle's second day, "Johnny Shiloh" was touted as a hero throughout the North, and was officially inducted into the regular army a month later in May 1862.

At Chickamauga, the 23rd Michigan was forced to retreat as Confederates overran the battlefield. Caught in the rebel advance, Johnny was run down by a Confederate colonel who shouted, "Surrender, you damned little Yankee!" Leveling his rifle at the officer, Clem quickly pulled the trigger, wounding the man and knocking him from his horse. Still, he was not out of danger, and gambled on playing dead until he could slip away after dark. It worked, and when he was reunited with his regiment, Clem was again commended for his bravery, this time getting a promotion to sergeant—at the age of 12!

Shortly after Chickamauga Clem was captured, and for two months, before being exchanged, he was paraded around as an example of the "babies" being sent to fight the rebels. His jacket and shoes were stolen, as well as his prized cap, which bore the holes of three musket balls. Later in the war a bullet finally found him, but only knicked his ear. He also was wounded in the hip by a shell fragment.

Clem returned home a hero after Lee's surrender, but the war had whetted his appetite for the military life. In 1871 he tried to enter West Point. Even though he was a seasoned battle veteran, his lack of formal education had caught up with him; he failed the entrance exams. "That was certainly hard luck," he later said. "What is the use of being a Civil War veteran, bearing honorable scars, if in one's old age—say 20—one is turned down by an unappreciative government?" Never one to give up easily, Clem took his problem to an old comrade-in-arms, President Grant. The great general did not hold a West Point education in high regard and apparently shared Clem's contention that battle experience was a valid substitute for the disciplines of the Academy. He promptly made Clem a second lieutenant.

Early in his career as an officer, Lt. Clem was sent to Texas,

Sergeant John Clem, age 12. The officer's belt, buckle, and hatband were affectations permitted the young hero. Credit: Library of Congress

where he was charged with keeping peace and upholding the law along the Mexican border. Once, he trailed a band of cattle rustlers who narrowly escaped across the Rio Grande into Mexico. Thinking they were home free, they jeered Clem and his men by making "sinister motions with their thumbs and fingers." Fed up, Clem ordered his men across the river, where they killed all the outlaws.

Clem rose to the rank of major general, certainly justifying Grant's estimation of his qualities as an officer. Always anxious to do his part for his country, he volunteered to go to France with Pershing's army in 1917, but President Wilson decided that Clem had already done enough. Although he might have been inclined to stow himself aboard a troop ship, this time Clem left the fighting to others, and retired to a quiet life in San Antonio. He was the last Civil War veteran to have been on active duty.

Suggested Reading:

James A. Rhodes and Dean Jauchius: *Johnny Shiloh*

Admiral George Dewey. The most popular man in America at the end of the 19th century, his face appeared on everything from shaving mugs and bath soap to walking canes and cuff links.

Credit: Library of Congress

George Dewey

Hero of Manila Bay

b. December 26, 1837 Montpelier, Vermont
d. January 16, 1917 Washington, D.C.
Washington Cathedral

> *O dewey was the morning*
> *Upon the first of May*
> *And Dewey was the Admiral*
> *Down in Manila Bay*
> *And dewey were the Regent's eyes,*
> *Them orbs of royal blue;*
> *And dewey feel discouraged?*
> *I dew not think we dew.*

Eugene F. Ware, 1898

O what a time it was! For four days the city of
New York hosted a celebration the likes of which the country
had never seen. Three and a half million people took part,
cheering and shouting and singing. On the Hudson, fireboats
angled jets of water in all directions, battleships fired blanks
into the sky, and spanking clean tugboats puttered up and
down in drill-team formations. Barges carried huge floats composed of prancing stallions, soaring eagles, and trumpeting
maidens. Fireworks mingled with searchlights dancing over the
city and hundreds of buildings were draped with flags and
bunting of red, white, and blue. Thirty architects and sculptors
contributed to a hundred foot high Triumphal Arch, modeled
after the Arc de Triomphe in Paris, which was erected in
Madison Square just for the occasion. John Philip Sousa's fabulous band led 30,000 soldiers and sailors along a seven-mile
parade route packed with onlookers. And from the Brooklyn
Bridge, thousands of light bulbs formed letters 36 feet high,
spelling out the reason for the incredible display: WELCOME
DEWEY. It was September 1899, and 17 months after destroy-
ing the Spanish fleet at Manila Bay, Admiral George Dewey
had finally come home.

Scarcely two years before, Dewey in his wildest dreams could never have envisioned such a reception in his honor. The United States had been at peace for over 30 years and his Navy career seemed destined to end quietly and anonymously. But the lengthy peace made Americans itchy for war, and when it finally happened, Dewey had the good fortune to be the right man in the right place at the right time.

A Green Mountain boy from Montpelier, Vermont, George Dewey went to the Naval Academy because appointments to West Point had all been filled. He graduated third in his class in 1858. As executive officer of a sidewheeler gunboat during the Civil War, Dewey impressed his captain with "unrivaled coolness and courage" under fire on the Mississippi River near New Orleans. In later years, the image of calm, capable leadership in battle lingered as a part of Dewey's reputation.

After the Civil War, Dewey's career was uneventful, there being no wars to fight. He rose steadily through the ranks but became increasingly frustrated over living out his military days without an opportunity to distinguish himself in battle. The ceremonial duties of showing the flag in foreign ports did little to relieve the frustration.

At home, Dewey was known as something of a society man, hobnobbing with the rich and famous as a member of the Metropolitan Club in Washington. He always dressed impeccably, rarely drank, and went horseback riding through the woods along Rock Creek every afternoon. At sea, there was another Dewey, known for his quick temper and strict discipline. If an early morning call for all hands on deck did not produce the entire crew, Dewey went below and tipped sleeping sailors out of their hammocks. In one incident, the crew of the sailing-steamer *Kearsarge* attempted a mutiny by remaining below decks, threatening to kill anyone who tried to come and get them. Pistols drawn, Dewey called through the hatch, "I am Mr. Dewey. I have two revolvers in my hands, and I'm going to shoot the first man who defies me." After a brief silence, the crew realized he was serious and the mutiny ended with every man filing out of the hold. Such encounters spawned numerous tales of Dewey's pistol-packing style of discipline among his crews, helping him to maintain order while at sea.

By the 1890s, the United States had reached its continental limits, but the urge for expansion persisted. European nations had colonies around the globe and many Americans wanted the United States to get a few of its own. In 1895, one senator told

Congress, "It is time that someone woke up and realized the necessity for annexing some property."

Spain had property: Puerto Rico, Cuba, the Philippines. Also, the Spanish were known for less than benevolent administration of their colonies. In an age of sensational, yellow journalism, the American press portrayed the Spanish as ruthless despots, fanning public outrage over alleged atrocities in the colonies. The stage was being set: America could liberate the Spanish possessions in a good cause, quenching the thirst for expansion at the same time. When the battleship *Maine* exploded and sank in Havana harbor on February 16, 1898, war was inevitable.

Meanwhile, America's future "Philippine Hero" became head of the Lighthouse Board in 1893. Edging ever closer to retirement, Dewey found no reward in lighthouse inspections. But things brightened a little in 1895 when he was made chief of the Board of Inspection. In that position, he supervised the outfitting of new, advanced battleships like the *Maine*, which were mostly steel and heavily armored. Still, time was running out, and in 1897 he sought one last sea assignment before retiring. Under Secretary of the Navy Teddy Roosevelt, who was a major proponent of war with somebody, pulled strings and got Dewey command of the Asiatic Squadron, based in Hong Kong.

Taking over the fleet in January 1898, Dewey didn't have long to wait before things started happening. Nine days after the *Maine* disaster he received a telegram from Roosevelt ordering him to hold the Spanish fleet, based in Manila, on the Asiatic coast. He spent the next two months preparing his fleet for battle, and then sailed for the Philippines on April 27, two days after war had been declared. As the ships steamed toward their rendezvous with the Spanish, an occasional shout was heard: "Remember the *Maine!*"

Before dawn on May 1, 1898, Dewey's squadron of six warships slipped into Manila Bay and was met by the outdated Spanish fleet. The tension was extraordinary—this was the biggest moment in American Naval history since the War of 1812. At 5:35 A.M. the United States was transformed from a growing nation into a world power when Commodore Dewey called down to his captain: "You may fire when you are ready, Gridley." A fury of cannon fire was unleashed on the enemy.

Two hours later, Dewey pulled his fleet out of the battle. He had been told that ammunition was running low and wanted to count exactly how much was left. The men in the gun turrets were dismayed—despite a thick screen of smoke obscuring their view of the Spanish ships, they knew things were going well. But a Navy with no ammunition seven thousand miles from home would be easy prey, so to keep secret the real reason for pulling back, the crews were told they were stopping for breakfast. This explanation also went out in news releases, and it contributed greatly to Dewey's heroic image after the war. Imagine! With the battle raging, the fleet commander had interrupted everything so his men could have their breakfast!

Dewey found that the report of low ammunition was wrong, and shortly after 11:00 A.M. he headed back at the enemy fleet. Or what was left of it. Except for three small gunboats, the Spanish squadron had been completely destroyed. The remainder was quickly sunk, and at 12:25 P.M. the Spanish surrendered. After a seven hour battle that included a 3½ hour pause for breakfast, Manila Bay belonged to Dewey, and at the cost of only eight men wounded.

When word of the overwhelming victory reached the United States, all the years of peace and tranquility ended in a frenzy of unabashed hero worship. The name "George Dewey" was attached to cats and dogs and newborn babies. Walking canes were topped by Dewey's head and there were Dewey ties, pins, and cuff links. His face appeared on shaving mugs, paper napkins, bath soap, and all sorts of toys. His bust adorned parlor tables, paintings of the triumph graced America's walls, and a swarm of giddy songs and poems filled the air. Imperialism had a wonderful, busting-out-all-over feeling about it, and George Dewey was its grandest symbol.

Dewey remained in the Philippines for a year, until the United States had secured control of the islands, and then sailed leisurely for home. The spectacular welcome in New York was followed by another in Washington, where Congress presented him with a golden sword and it was declared that Dewey had "demonstrated the supremacy of American sea power and transferred to the United States an imperial cluster of islands of the Pacific."

The rank of Admiral of the Navy, which only Farragut and Porter had held previously, was resurrected for Dewey, and he was considered a presidential possibility until his political ignorance became obvious. Uncomfortable as a superstar, Dewey irritated his legions of admirers by taking great pains to avoid the press. His popular image dulled further when he deeded a house given him by the public to his wife only months after he had received it. But Dewey didn't want the house, and didn't feel any obligation to keep it. When the press finally left him alone and his stardom faded, Dewey was much happier. He spent his last years in Washington, where he actively enjoyed the social whirl of the capital city.

Suggested Reading:

Richard S. West, Jr.: *Admirals of American Empire*
Laurin Hall Healy and Luis Kutner: *The Admiral*

Wild Bill Donovan

Spymaster

b. January 1, 1883 Buffalo, New York
d. February 8, 1959 Washington, D.C.
Arlington

War isn't what it used to be. Once, armies of foot-soldiers faced off in bloody exchanges only to gain or lose a wheatfield or a stand of trees. Each yard was dearly earned. Now, war is a matter of clandestine campaigns and technological espionage; the victories are subtle and unannounced. William J. "Wild Bill" Donovan was a unique man who excelled, perhaps more than anyone ever will, at both forms of warfare. Called by *The New York Times* "a living symbol of what we think of as pure, simple, unadulterated courage," Donovan was one of our most decorated combat heroes of World War I. And then, a quarter century later, he created from scratch the Office of Strategic Services (OSS), a secret intelligence service that was involved in every theater of World War II, playing a vital role in the Allied victory.

America's spymaster had his first taste of undercover activities when he was growing up in Buffalo, New York. Catholic refugees from Ireland regularly found their way to safety and shelter among the Donovan clan, slipping across Lake Erie from Canada in darkness and later disappearing into a hopeful future in the New World. The restrained emotion and cautious whispering that characterized these brief acquaintances indelibly marked Will's behavior, and anyone who knew him as an adult was impressed by the control and soft-spoken delivery of "Wild Bill" Donovan.

So why the nickname if he was so un-"wild"? The short, stout Donovan left a prospering law practice to become a part of General John J. Pershing's army, first along the Mexican border hunting for Pancho Villa, and then as an infantry officer in France in World War I. He felt strongly that a fit army would prevail in the toughest going, and constantly exercised his troops with that in mind. Long hikes with full gear were typical of Donovan's style, with himself leading the way, setting the example. His theory proved true in battle after battle, and it was once said, by a priest, that "his men would have cheerfully gone to hell with him." But there was one holdout, one soldier who was not convinced. After constant harassment from his regiment buddies, the soldier reluctantly conceded, "Wild Bill is a son of a bitch, but he's a game one." The nickname was picked up by the press, and by the end of the war everyone was using it.

Donovan's performance in action gave newspapers ample opportunity to popularize his name. He was quickly recognized as one of the best field commanders among the Allied forces, and once received a letter from Teddy Roosevelt in which the former president related how one of his own sons longed to serve under him. "My boys regard you as about the finest example of the American fighting man," wrote Roosevelt, who no doubt shared the sentiment. Donovan combined tactical savvy, thorough training, cold nerve, and a genuine enthusiasm for combat in leading his men to successive advances, sometimes moving so fast that the Americans had to come back and round up prisoners at the end of a day's fighting. The poet Joyce Kilmer, one of Donovan's sergeants, wrote that he would rather remain a sergeant under Wild Bill than be "a lieutenant in any other regiment in the world."

During the Meuse-Argonne offensive in 1918, Donovan once rallied his troops into battle, but heavy fire sent the men scurrying for cover. Unperturbed, Donovan stood his ground in the open studying a field map while enemy bullets killed the dirt all around him. Astonished, his men heard him say, "See, they can't hit me, and they won't hit you!" Wild Bill's indifference to danger was infectious, turning many a fearful recruit into a courageous soldier. He emerged from the war a bona fide hero, winner of the Medal of Honor, the Legion of Honor (France), and the Purple Heart with two Oak Leaf Clusters, among others.

Between wars, Donovan mingled public service with his law practice. He was an assistant attorney general under Calvin Coolidge and was considered as a running mate for Herbert Hoover in 1928, but his Catholicism was still 30 years from political acceptance. In 1935, Donovan went to Rome as a private citizen and toyed with Mussolini's pride so cleverly that Il Duce personally granted him an inspection of the "new" Italian army that was preparing to attack Ethiopia. The first outsider to get a look at Mussolini's army, and on a guided tour no less,

Donovan discovered that it was much stronger than anyone in Washington had imagined. The episode revealed Donovan's talent as an actor, but more importantly, it demonstrated his ability to get information that somebody else didn't necessarily want to give away.

In 1940, England was under heavy attack from the Germans, and many officials in the U.S. government had given up hope that the British could avoid defeat. Bill Donovan thought otherwise, and secretly went to England to assess the situation. Sir William Stephenson, better known as the super-spy "Intrepid," has called this trip "one of the most momentous missions ever undertaken by an agent in the history of western civilization." Donovan found that the British had the heart and will to repulse the Nazis, but they were sorely in need of ships and munitions. Within weeks of his return to Washington, he had persuaded President Roosevelt to provide the aid, and 50 ships were on the way. Without them, D-Day might have taken place on the beaches of England.

Donovan's ability to come up with much-needed strategic information helped make Roosevelt aware of the importance of an intelligence-gathering network, and in 1941 the President asked Donovan to plan such a service that would be effective on a world-wide scale. In 1942, the Office of Strategic Services was born from this plan, and Donovan was made its director.

Within months, America's first "cloak and dagger" army was operating behind the scenes in all corners of the globe, with Wild Bill Donovan darting from continent to continent coordinating its activities. For three years, the exploits of this legendary spy network, which have inspired countless books and movies, ranged from daring missions of sabotage and rescue to the purchase of ball bearings desperately needed by the Nazi war machine. Winston Churchill considered maps of war zones produced by the OSS to be the most reliable. Underground resistance movements depended on OSS for almost everything, from food and clothing to weapons and money. In one case, a wild Burmese jungle tribe, whose diet included monkeys, was organized and trained to fight the Japanese.

Donovan's secret army attracted a diverse and talented group of idealists and adventurers, many of whom rose to postwar notoriety. Among them were Arthur Goldberg, Arthur Schlesinger, Jr., Sterling Hayden, Julia Child, John Birch, Allen Dulles, and President Reagan's CIA director, William J. Casey.

At war's end, the OSS was disbanded. Before returning to

his law firm, Donovan was a member of the prosecution team at the Nuremberg trials. The OSS had obtained most of the crucial documents to be used in the trials, but Donovan preferred that the Nazis should be found guilty by the German people rather than by a court of war victors. He was rebuffed in his attempts to arrange such trials, and quit the prosecution because of it.

Donovan had advocated a permanent intelligence service before the end of the war, knowing that the era of open warfare was giving way to a new age of secret operations. In 1947, the Central Intelligence Agency (CIA) was created to do at all times what the OSS had done during World War II. Today Wild Bill Donovan's portrait hangs inside the entrance to CIA headquarters, signifying his place as father of America's world of spies, secret agents, deception, and intrigue.

Suggested Reading:

Anthony Cave Brown: *The Last Hero: Wild Bill Donovan*
Richard Dunlop: *Donovan: America's Master Spy*

Abner Doubleday

Benched Inventor of Baseball

b. June 26, 1819 Ballston Spa, New York
d. January 26, 1893 Mendham, New Jersey
Arlington

Oh! somewhere in this favored land the sun is shining bright;
The band is playing somewhere, and somewhere hearts are light.
And somewhere men are laughing, and somewhere children shout;
But there is no joy in Mudville—mighty Casey has Struck Out.

"Casey at the Bat" by Ernest L. Thayer

Chances are, if you take a mobile tour of Arlington National Cemetery, the guide will point out the grave of General Abner Doubleday and then describe him as the "inventor of baseball." Everyone on the bus will look to the left and search for the stone, filled with the warmth of knowing that our national pastime was pulled out of thin air by a red-blooded American who was also a career military man. It's just so right, that baseball should come from the mind of a patriot, and it's just what Albert G. Spalding wanted everyone to believe.

Yes, Albert G. Spalding. Former baseball star, head of the huge sporting goods company, and fiercely nationalistic American. So fierce, in fact, that the idea that baseball might have come from anywhere other than the United States was practically treason in his mind.

At the turn of the century, there was too much talk about baseball's having derived from the British games of rounders and cricket. Spalding decided to squash such talk forever by appointing a fact-finding commission that would set the record straight. Since Spalding orchestrated the exercise, there wasn't much doubt about the outcome. In 1907, the commission concluded that "baseball had its origins in the United States" and that it "was devised by Abner Doubleday at Cooperstown, New York in 1839." The only supporting evidence came from 73-year-old Abner Graves, who claimed to have been Doubleday's playmate at Cooperstown. Actually, Doubleday was about to enter West Point when Graves was born, so it is improbable that Graves would have seen young Abner sketch "with a stick in the dirt the present diamond-shaped Base Ball field." Also, Doubleday was at West Point, not Cooperstown, throughout 1839, and among his voluminous writings, including 67 diaries, there is not a single mention of baseball. But since Doubleday had died in 1893, he could neither acknowledge nor refute the claim, and over the years, with a lot of help from the people in Cooperstown and organized baseball, he became the inventor of our national game. And Spalding made a fortune selling bats and balls and gloves.

You might be interested in knowing a little about Abner Doubleday anyway. He rode with Zachary Taylor in the Mexican War (1846–48), saw action in the Seminole Wars in Florida (1856–58), and was on hand at Fort Sumter, South Carolina, when it was bombarded by seceding Confederates. By ordering a return of cannon fire, he is credited with having fired the first shot for the North in the Civil War. He fought in the crucial battles of Antietam, Fredericksburg, and Chancellorsville. At Gettysburg, Doubleday's men beat back Pickett's charge, "thereby saving the battle and the Union." A bronze statue commemorates his heroism there.

Doubleday was not particularly well liked. He was "outspoken, verbose and critical," and some relatives felt the day was ruined if Uncle Abner dropped in for a visit. After his feats at Gettysburg, Doubleday's arrogance may have contributed to General Meade's decision to send him to manage a warehouse in Buffalo, New York. Luckily, President Lincoln stepped in and had him assigned to a more dignified post. In 1873, Doubleday retired from the Army, and as far as anyone knows, he wasn't much of a baseball fan.

After the National Baseball Museum was erected in Cooperstown, and after Abner Doubleday became as familiar as "Play Ball!", the true origins of the game resurfaced. No, Doubleday did not invent it. Yes, it is derived from those British ball games. Numerous books and articles have relegated poor ol' Abner to the bleachers of baseball history, all the encyclopedias have echoed the sad news, and eventually the tour guides will hear about it, too.

Suggested Reading:

Harold Peterson: *The Man Who Invented Baseball*

Peggy Eaton

Scandal

b. December 3, 1799 Washington City
d. November 8, 1879 Washington, D.C.
Oak Hill

Female virtue is like a tender and delicate flower; let but the breath of suspicion rest upon it, and it withers and perhaps perishes forever.

Andrew Jackson

One of the most entertaining stories of early Washington is that of Peggy Eaton, the daughter of a local tavern keeper. Scandalous gossip about this bright and captivating woman, whom a popular poet christened "the most beautiful woman in America," caused a brouhaha that stands as one of the silliest episodes in American history. At the time, it was a very serious matter. Social and governmental life in the Capital came to a standstill, forcing President Andrew Jackson to dismiss his entire cabinet. And in the end, the tempest surrounding Peggy Eaton determined Jackson's successor to the White House.

When the seat of the federal government was moved from Philadelphia to the District of Columbia in 1800, the new capital offered very little in the way of lodging. William O'Neale's inn and tavern became the Washington address of most of the senators and congressmen, who were forced to leave their families in their home states. O'Neale's daughter Peggy, who was born at the inn, grew up calling the most influential men in America "uncle," and each night a different one propped her on his knee and told her a bedtime story.

By the time she was 17, Peggy had developed into an attractive young girl, with dark eyes, an ample bust, and cascades of rich brown hair. She possessed a lightning wit and a talent to tease, but acquired an occasionally profane tongue, having grown up within earshot of the tavern's drinking men. Alluring, playful, and a tad saucy, Peggy drew countless offers of marriage, but left most suitors brooding in their ale.

In 1817, after a romance of less than a month, Peggy suddenly married John Timberlake, a seafaring businessman. At about the same time, John Eaton, a wealthy Tennessee lawyer and a protégé of General Andrew Jackson, took up residence at the O'Neale inn. Mrs. Timberlake started spending time with Mr. Eaton when her husband went to sea early in 1821, more time than seemed proper for a young wife with her husband gone and a daughter in tow. The two were seen together at social gatherings and strolling lazily through parks. They took long, unchaperoned carriage rides. Word circulated that they were having an affair, but when Timberlake came home in the fall, everything seemed to return to normal and the talk subsided.

In 1823, Timberlake set sail on a voyage that would have him out of Washington for four years. Peggy showed herself pregnant shortly afterward. She also rekindled her apparent intimacy with John Eaton. This was more than many of Washington's citizens could endure, and this time the reaction was more than whispered gossip. Peggy's name disappeared from invitation lists and on the eve of her own parties, groups of invited women would contract mysterious illnesses that kept them away. Just beneath the surface of social Washington, a movement was on to ignore her existence.

In 1826, news reached Washington that John Timberlake had died at sea. If illness was the actual cause, no one in the Capital wanted to believe it. The preferred, and readily accepted, rumor was that Timberlake had finally learned of his wife's infidelity and had slit his throat in despair.

The icing was on the cake when the widowed Mrs. Timberlake became Mrs. Eaton on January 1, 1829.

Now enters Andrew Jackson, hero of the Battle of New Orleans and newly elected President of the United States. Jackson came to Washington having just lost his wife, Rachel, whom he idolized. He had married Rachel when she thought the divorce from her first husband had been finalized, but she was mistaken, and a cloud of vile rumor had followed her for the rest of her life. As far as Jackson was concerned, rumor and gossip had driven poor Rachel to her grave, and with the bitterness of her death fresh in his heart and mind, Jackson saw Peggy Eaton as a victim of the same unscrupulous tongues. Once provoked, he was determined to defend her.

In late winter of 1829, Jackson set about forming his administration. John C. Calhoun was his vice president and the pre-

Peggy Eaton: "I am not a saint." Credit: Library of Congress

sumed successor to the presidency. Little known Martin Van Buren, the crafty governor of New York, was named secretary of state, and Jackson's long-time friend and supporter, John Eaton, became secretary of war.

Immediately after the cabinet appointments were announced, a furor arose over the appearance of John Eaton's name on the list. The critics were numerous and unanimous in their objection: no man should hold a high government office while married to a woman of such low moral standards. In the midst of the uproar, Jackson received a letter from a Reverend Ezra

Stiles Ely. According to Ely, Peggy had bedded more than a few men in her time, her children were not fathered by John Timberlake, and she had miscarried a pregnancy when her husband had been away for more than nine months. In addition, the preacher claimed that the President's own beloved wife had been among those who found Peggy wanting in virtue.

Jackson considered the letter as ruthless and unfounded as the gossip that had killed his Rachel. He would not stand for it, and began collecting affidavits echoing his judgment that Mrs. Eaton was "as chaste as a virgin." (It is not known how many jobs in Jackson's administration hinged on presenting one of these proclamations of virtue.) With so many Washington hostesses refusing to accept Peggy into their homes, Jackson literally ordered his cabinet members to attend White House dinners. Anyone whose wife did not come along could expect serious consequences.

Martin Van Buren had no trouble attending—he was a widower. He also made a clever assessment of his chief executive: supporting Peggy Eaton could lead to more than just presidential friendship. Van Buren held parties in Peggy's honor and let it be known that he stood firmly with the President on this "issue." On the other hand, Vice President Calhoun joined his wife in ostracizing Mrs. Eaton. Jackson began to distance himself from Calhoun, and the one-time front-runner saw his presidential hopes vanish. By the time Jackson left office, Van Buren had propelled himself into Old Hickory's favor on the hem of the "petticoat war," and then succeeded Jackson as President.

For more than a year, social Washington was somber, to say the least. Couples were compelled to attend parties notable for awkward tensions and crowds of women disappearing into the powder room whenever the War Secretary's wife arrived. Marital relationships suffered because men continued to fall under the spell of Peggy's beauty and wit. By the spring of 1831, the social situation had practically dragged the government to a halt, and just about everyone longed for a change. Jackson could no longer command people to be friendly, nor could he convince anyone of Peggy's untainted moral character. It was time for drastic action. Following a scheme devised by Van Buren, Jackson dissolved his cabinet, eliminating the Eaton migraine from his administration. It was a move unique in our history: the highest officials in government resigned in no small part because their wives despised a more beautiful woman. Almost immediately Washington came to life again and the government was able to concentrate on more important matters.

In the aftermath, John Eaton was appointed minister to Spain. In Madrid, far removed from her Washington reputation, Peggy found the approval she had been denied in her home town and was treated like a real lady. The queen was especially fond of her, taking her in as a confidant. Peggy practiced the Spanish art of teasing with a fan and shared with the queen an affection for cigars. The two women frequently locked the palace doors to enjoy an undisturbed smoke.

John Eaton died in 1856. Back in Washington and a widow again, Peggy occupied herself with care of her orphaned granddaughters. In 1858, she agreed to let their impoverished Italian dance instructor, Antonio Buchignani, live in her house. Peggy was now almost 60 and Buchignani was not yet 20, so her friends were dumbstruck when they heard that the two were married in June of 1859. Again unwelcome in many homes, Peggy and her dancing husband lived unobtrusively in town until the Civil War ended. In 1865, one of her granddaughters secretly began an affair with Buchignani. They conspired to relieve Peggy of more than half her considerable wealth, and then boarded a steamer for Europe. Before long, Peggy learned that her granddaughter had given birth to a child fathered by _her_ husband.

Although humiliated, Peggy O'Neale Timberlake Eaton Buchignani recovered in time. She divorced the dancer and reclaimed Eaton as her last name. By 1870, few people in the Capital remembered the events of 1829–31, so in her seventies Peggy happily entertained younger folk with tales of early Washington. She had always maintained that she was the first child born in the nation's capital, and she garnished that claim with stories that marked her as the best and oldest source of the city's history. She attended sessions of Congress regularly, a habit she had begun at the age of five. Just before she died, Peggy half-jokingly suggested that her epitaph read "she was never dull." Her request went unfulfilled, but not for the statement's lack of accuracy.

Suggested Reading:

Queena Pollack: _Peggy Eaton_
Leon Phillips: _That Eaton Woman_

Medgar Evers

Civil Rights Leader

> b. June 2, 1925 Decatur, Mississippi
> d. June 12, 1963 Jackson, Mississippi
> Arlington

On June 11, 1963, Governor George Wallace stood on the steps of the University of Alabama in an unsuccessful attempt to prevent racial integration of the school. That evening President Kennedy spoke to the nation on television, advocating "equal rights and equal opportunities" for all Americans. Medgar Wiley Evers, Mississippi field secretary of the NAACP, watched the address and then spoke at a rally in Jackson. Just after midnight, as he was walking to the front door of his house, a sniper's bullet ripped into his back. He died within an hour. Virtually unknown outside Mississippi before his death, Evers became a martyred hero to the cause of civil rights, his life a symbol of courage and determination in the face of constant racial harassment.

A veteran of the Normandy invasion, Evers graduated from Alcorn A & M College in 1952, became a salesman for a black-owned insurance company, and joined the NAACP. In 1954, he became the association's first Mississippi field secretary, traveling throughout the state building NAACP membership, organizing voter registration drives, and helping parents file desegregation petitions in local school districts. James Meredith, the first black admitted to the University of Mississippi, considered Evers's bravery vital to his successful enrollment. Whenever blacks were abused Evers investigated, and in the case of the murder of 14-year-old Emmett Till in 1955, he disguised himself as a farm laborer to gather information. His files of affidavits charging white cruelty to blacks stand now as a record of racial hatred in America.

By June 1963, Evers had long been "the heartbeat of any integration activity in the state of Mississippi." His campaign for equal employment opportunities and desegregation of all public facilities in Jackson was in full swing. There were daily marches, rallies, and pressure on city officials, and a black

Medgar Evers. Credit: NAACP

consumer boycott had crippled the city's white-owned businesses. Abruptly, with a bullet from the same model high-powered rifle that would kill John Kennedy five months later, Evers's crusade was over. But the tension in Jackson exploded across the country in riots and violence, signaling the start of the active struggle for racial equality in the South.

Evers was well aware of the dangers of his work. He accepted it and forged ahead, maintaining that "if I die it will be in a good cause. I've been fighting for America just as much as the soldiers in Viet Nam." He was buried with full military honors in Arlington National Cemetery, his gravestone facing across the Potomac River toward the Lincoln Memorial.

Byron de la Beckwith, a fertilizer salesman, was twice tried for the murder of Medgar Evers. Both trials ended with hung juries (all white) and he was released. In 1975, Beckwith was convicted of illegally transporting a ticking time bomb into Louisiana, allegedly destined for the New Orleans home of a Jewish community leader.

On the morning of June 12, 1983, 20 years after Medgar Evers's death, thousands of people were gathered along the banks of the Potomac River near Arlington Cemetery. At the same time, a small group held a memorial service at Evers's graveside. Those along the river probably were unaware of this 20th anniversary; they had come out to view the first ever Capital fly-over by the Space Shuttle, the latest symbol of our progress in space exploration. Those at Evers's grave talked of progress, too. They told how the "spirit" of Medgar Evers had changed the South. How ten thousand registered black voters in Mississippi, remarkable in 1963, had swelled to four hundred thousand 20 years later. How his spirit had carried the civil rights struggle through its darkest hours and how it would continue to inspire in years to come.

As that magnificent Space Shuttle flew by, piggy-backed on a 747 jetliner, it was impossible not to make the connection: In 20 years, Americans had come a long way. The mysteries of space had gradually yielded to hard work and dreams; so too had "justice for all." And in both fields, there was still more progress to be made.

As the memorial service came to an end, the small group joined voices in singing the "Ode to Medgar Evers:"

Tell me, tell me, why was Medgar Evers born?
Tell me, tell me, why was Medgar Evers born?
Somebody had to hold our hands,
Somebody had to take a stand,
Somebody had to develop the land,
And that's why Medgar Evers was born.

Suggested Reading:

Myrlie B. Evers: *For Us, the Living*

F. Scott Fitzgerald

Author

b. September 24, 1896 St. Paul, Minnesota
d. December 21, 1940 Hollywood, California
St. Mary's

So we beat on, boats against the current, borne back ceaselessly into the past.

The Great Gatsby

When F. Scott Fitzgerald was in college he told a friend, "I want to be one of the greatest writers that ever lived, don't you?" Strong words for a young man not yet 20. But Scott was serious. He believed not only that an American could do anything, he believed an American could do <u>everything</u>. Together, Scott and Zelda Fitzgerald set out to try. Their roller-coaster ride through the 20s—the Jazz Age—was a wild attempt to create, experience, and record the high life of an entire generation. Were they successful? Part triumph and part tragedy, the story of the Fitzgeralds is one of the main chapters in the history of modern American literature.

Although he was born and reared in Minnesota, Fitzgerald had strong family ties to Maryland, which throughout his life served him as a symbol of permanence and stability. His family tree included not only Francis Scott Key, author of the "Star Spangled Banner," but also Mary Surratt, hanged for conspiring to murder Abraham Lincoln.

Educated at private schools and at Princeton, Scott spent his college career writing, drinking, and struggling for passing grades. In 1917 he dropped out to join the Army. He was no better at soldiering than he had been at studying, however, and was later remembered as "the world's worst second lieutenant."

At a dance in Montgomery, Alabama, where Scott was stationed, he first met Zelda Sayre, the radiant, honey-blonde daughter of a local judge. Zelda's reputation as a fun-loving free spirit caused army pilots to fly stunts over her house to impress her. Flirtatious and impulsive, she was also intelligent

Zelda Sayre Fitzgerald

Spirit of the Jazz Age

b. July 24, 1900 Montgomery, Alabama
d. March 11, 1948 Asheville, North Carolina
St. Mary's

and ambitious. For a husband she wanted someone who could give her glamour and fame. Scott, with his own Adonis-like good looks, courted her ardently, and soon they were engaged.

Following his discharge, Scott went to New York hoping to strike it rich with a book he had been writing in the officer's club on weekends. In March 1920, Scribners published *This Side of Paradise*, "a novel about flappers, written for philosophers," and the 23-year-old Fitzgerald was launched on his meteoric career.

Roughly autobiographical (as is most of his work), the book is a testament to youthful revolt. Fitzgerald's depiction of life at Princeton—of petting parties, flirts, and vamps—shocked the Victorian parents of his generation but boosted sales. Newspapers reported that young girls used it as an instruction book. The $18,000 it earned during the first months enabled Scott to marry Zelda and start a ten-year spree of riotous living.

It was the Roaring Twenties and the Fitzgeralds were celebrities. Fueled by bathtub gin, they rode on the roofs of taxis, jumped into fountains, and presided over endless rounds of parties. After one particularly memorable weekend, they posted house rules:

Visitors are requested not to break down doors in search of liquor, even when authorized to do so by the host and hostess.

Guests are respectfully notified that invitations to stay over Monday, issued by the host and hostess during the small hours of Sunday morning, must not be taken seriously.

Looking back, Scott wrote:

I remember riding in a taxi one afternoon between very tall buildings under a mauve and rosy sky; I began to bawl because I had everything I wanted and knew I would never be so happy again.

Fitzgerald quickly followed his first success with several collections of short stories and another novel, *The Beautiful and Damned*. Again, the tale was loosely modeled on the dissolute life of Scott and Zelda. Indeed, Zelda claimed the book contained material from an old diary which had mysteriously disappeared after her marriage.

When *The Great Gatsby* appeared in 1925, the reviewers were almost unanimous in their praise; Fitzgerald was hailed as a modern master. Fable-like in construction, the book is an investigation of the American Dream. In his confusion over love and money, Jay Gatsby is tragically destroyed. The detail is brilliant; Gatsby's Rolls Royce represents his own glittering surface:

It was a rich cream color, bright with nickel, swollen here and there in its monstrous length with triumphant hat-boxes and supper-boxes and tool-boxes, and terraced with a labyrinth of windshields that mirrored a dozen suns.

But although *Gatsby* was a hit with the critics, sales were slow.

The 1929 stock market crash signaled the end of the party for Scott and Zelda. During the 20s they had racked up huge physical and emotional debts; they spent the 30s paying them off.

In 1930, Zelda suffered a nervous breakdown and was hospitalized. The cause, according to the doctors, was a combination of heavy drinking and the strain of living with Scott. The years of dazzling exhibitionism had only masked Zelda's growing insanity. Though deeply, romantically in love, they were both headstrong and competitive. In an attempt to establish her own identity, Zelda had taken up ballet and, against Scott's wishes, was writing fiction.

During six weeks in a Baltimore hospital, Zelda completed *Save Me the Waltz*, her own account of life with Scott. Zelda called the book "none of Scott's damn business," but he was outraged at the thinly disguised portrait of himself as a drunk, and insisted on major revisions. Initially treated as a curiosity, *Save Me the Waltz* is now generally viewed as the product of an original but frustrated talent.

Ironically, Scott, living in Towson, Maryland, was then in the midst of writing *Tender is the Night* and drawing heavily on the effect Zelda's precarious mental health was having on their relationship. In the book, a psychiatrist exhausts his own emotional resources while trying to cure a patient. The novel received mixed reviews, but for the rest of his life Fitzgerald was convinced it was his best work. Zelda enjoyed it because it evoked memories of their early happiness together. Sadly, memories were all the Fitzgeralds had now. When Zelda's condition grew worse, Scott grieved. "I left my capacity for hoping," he wrote, "on the little roads that led to Zelda's sanitarium."

In an effort to recoup his financial losses, Scott moved alone to Hollywood in 1937 to devote himself to screenwriting. There he met Sheila Graham, a newspaper columnist who, for awhile, had a stabilizing influence on him. Keeping him from parties and alcohol, she made it possible for Scott to focus his energy one last time. With the exception of some important contributions to *Gone With the Wind*, Scott's film scripts were generally mediocre. However, in 1939 he carefully planned and began an ambitious new novel telling the inside story of the movie industry. In October 1940, he wrote Zelda, "I am deep in the novel, living it, and it makes me happy." The Saturday before Christmas, Fitzgerald was reading a magazine and eating a chocolate bar. Suddenly he rose from the chair, grabbed the mantle, and then collapsed. He was 44. *The Last Tycoon*, the book he had pinned his hopes on, was unfinished.

Zelda took the news of Scott's death with remarkable calm and arranged to have his body sent to Maryland. Scott had once written of the state:

I belong here, where everything is civilized and gay and rotted and polite. And I wouldn't mind a bit if in a few years Zelda and I could snuggle up together under a stone in some old graveyard here. That is really a happy thought and not melancholy at all.

Because he was not a practicing Catholic he was refused burial in the family plot at St. Mary's Churchyard, and was buried instead at nearby Rockville Union Cemetery.

Zelda, living at Highland Hospital in Asheville, North Carolina, painted, wrote, and took long walks. Though Scott had died in relative obscurity, she predicted he would one day be honored as a major author. She didn't have long to wait. When an edited version of *The Last Tycoon* was published in 1941, Stephen Vincent Benet was reverential:

You can take off your hats now, gentlemen, and I think perhaps you had better. This is not a legend, this is a reputation—and, seen in perspective, it may well be one of the most secure reputations of our time.

Seven years later, a fire swept through the building at Highland where Zelda was living. Six women were trapped on the top floor; Zelda was one of them. Fulfilling Scott's wistful remark from long before, she was buried with him in Rockville.

In 1975, permission was granted to move the Fitzgeralds to the Catholic cemetery. In a written statement, the Archbishop of Washington described Fitzgerald as "an artist who was able with lucidity and poetic imagination to portray the struggle between grace and death." Fitzgerald had not only portrayed the struggle; he and Zelda had <u>lived</u> it. Their own unsettling story is one of the best documents we have of what it was like to be young, famous, and in love during the first half of the 20th century.

Suggested Reading:

Sara Mayfield: *Exiles From Paradise: Zelda and Scott Fitzgerald*
Nancy Milford: *Zelda: A Biography*
Matthew Bruccoli: *Some Sort of Epic Grandeur: The Life of F. Scott Fitzgerald*

Joseph Gales

Editor, Publisher

b. April 10, 1786 Eckington, England
d. July 21, 1860 Washington, D.C.
Congressional

*The one name that stands out with the clearest prominence as the
exemplar of the best journalism during the first half of the last century
is that of Joseph Gales.*

The Washington Post, 1901

On a cold, damp day in January 1830, Daniel
Webster entered a packed senate chamber to deliver the most
emotionally charged speech of his career. Senator Robert
Hayne of South Carolina had confronted him—and a still
young United States—with a critical question: Where does the
authority of the individual states cease and that of the national
government begin? Webster's reply would reach down to the
very core of his beliefs. Sensing the importance of this historic
moment, he summoned the most prominent journalist in America, Joseph Gales, to personally record it.

Gales was the editor and publisher of the *National Intelligencer*, the first daily newspaper in the nation's capital. In an
era before press conferences and the evening news, the *Intelligencer* was the channel through which administration policy
was carried to the people. It also carried transcripts of congressional debates and Gales's editorials, frequently the leading
commentary on important issues of the day.

A native of England but raised mostly in Philadelphia and
Raleigh, North Carolina, Gales learned stenography from his
father, also a journalist. He was hired as a congressional reporter for the *Intelligencer* in 1807, and became its sole editor
and publisher three years later at the age of 24.

At first intimidated by the likes of James Monroe, John
Quincy Adams, and James Madison, who doubted his capabilities and experience, Gales soon earned advisory status

Joseph Gales's shorthand notes of the climactic end of Daniel Webster's reply to Hayne in 1830. Credit: Boston Public Library

with his astute editorials. Early in 1812, he led the campaign to arouse public sentiment against Britain's control of the seas, which was stifling American trade. "They violate the rights, and wound deeply the best interests, of the whole American people," he wrote. "If we yield to them, at this time, the cause may be considered as abandoned." The cause became the War of 1812.

By openly denouncing the land of his birth, Gales lost his newspaper, at least temporarily. Admiral George Cockburn, who commanded the British capture of Washington in August 1814, sought out the offices of the *Intelligencer*. He ordered the presses destroyed, the newspaper's reference collection burned along the canal (now Constitution Avenue), and all the c's in the type case destroyed so that Gales couldn't print anything nasty about him later on! A witness to the event quoted the haughty Cockburn: "Well, good people, I do not wish to injure you, but I really am afraid my friend Josey (Gales) will be affronted with me, if after burning Jemmy's palace (Madison's White House) I do not pay him the same compliment—so my lads, take your axes, pull down the house and burn the papers in the street."

On December 2, 1823, President Monroe made a lengthy speech to Congress detailing his policy toward foreign meddling in the New World. The next day, the *Intelligencer* carried the text of the speech on a back page under the simple heading "President's Message." It was the first publication of what would be known years later as the Monroe Doctrine.

In 1827, Gales came out strongly against Andrew Jackson for the presidency, citing, among other things, his ruthless execution of six men for insubordination. After Jackson won the election, the *Intelligencer* was dropped as the official courier of government news for the first time since 1800, losing critical federal subsidies in the process. Forced to develop an added source of income, Gales and his brother-in-law, William W. Seaton, secured a contract from Congress in 1832 to produce the *American State Papers*, a compilation of important Congressional documents covering everything from foreign relations and Indian affairs to commerce and the Post Office. Comprising 38 volumes, the *Papers* are considered the most valuable historical record of U.S. affairs in the period between the Revolution and the Civil War.

On top of his reputation as a journalist, Joseph Gales was well known for his generosity. He gave money freely to those in need, even if it meant giving away all that he had in his pockets. Once, on a freezing day, he put five dollars in Anne Royall's hand and told her to buy some warm shoes. When she was hard-pressed to buy paper to print her own journal, Gales ordered his printers to give her as much paper as she needed, free of charge.

Without the *Intelligencer's* first-hand transcriptions of congressional debates, many of the great speeches of Webster, Clay, Calhoun, and others would have been lost forever. The greatest of these is certainly Webster's historic encounter with Senator Hayne, often called the Great Debate of 1830. Hayne had argued well that the states were not bound to accept all things handed down by the federal government: a federal law that might benefit a northern state should not be forced on a southern state; the bonds of the Union were secondary to the liberty of the states. To Webster, placing states' liberty above the well-being of the nation as a whole would insure the dissolution of a "once glorious Union." With Gales copying his words on narrow strips of paper, Webster addressed the Congress. Building to an impassioned climax, he proclaimed "Liberty and Union, now and forever, one and inseparable!" Thirty years later, Abraham Lincoln took inspiration from those words in his efforts to preserve the Union.

Gales copied down Webster's speech in shorthand and later transcribed it with the aid of his wife, Sarah. Because Webster was to insist on revising the speech several times, even years later, it is fortunate that Gales's shorthand report and the transcription were preserved, giving us what must be considered the most accurate account of what was actually said. It is curious that Webster felt he could improve on his original delivery. None of his revisions possesses the immediacy nor the brilliance of the emotional, extemporaneously spoken words preserved in the Gales transcription.

As the country edged toward civil war, a sensationalized style of writing began to dominate the nation's newspapers. The quiet dignity and eloquence of Gales and the *National Intelligencer* were fast becoming an anachronism. With Webster's words "Liberty and Union, now and forever, one and inseparable!" bannered across the top of the *Intelligencer* and two-thirds of its circulation in the South, where few agreed with that statement, the demise of what had been America's finest newspaper was inevitable. In a way, the *Intelligencer* was a chronicle of our second generation of patriots, those who shaped the post-revolutionary United States. Gales preserved many of the grandest moments of that generation. When he died in 1860, the last of that era passed with him. On the day of his funeral in a rare display for a newspaper man, many buildings in the city were draped in black, and schools and businesses were closed.

Suggested Reading:

William E. Ames: *A History of the National Intelligencer*

Alexander Gardner

Civil War Photographer

b. October 17, 1821 Paisley, Scotland
d. December 10, 1882 Washington, D.C.
Glenwood

When thinking of Civil War photography, the name Mathew Brady comes quickly to mind; Alexander Gardner is a vague association, at best. Well into this century Brady was routinely credited with most photography of the Civil War period, as if he were the only man who had had a camera. But if you have seen photographs of the gruesome corpses at Antietam and Gettysburg, the incredible weariness in the face of the "Last Lincoln," or the gallows images of the Lincoln conspirators, you have seen not the work of the fame-hungry Mathew Brady, but that of the hardworking Alexander Gardner.

A native of Glasgow, Scotland, Gardner was more interested in the welfare of man than in photography when he first visited the United States in 1849. He had come to establish a utopian commune in Iowa which stressed equal distribution of work and shared education of children by the adult community. After getting the settlement under way, Gardner returned to Glasgow where he continued to lecture and write on his ideas.

At the London World's Fair in 1851, Gardner may have met the famous Mathew Brady and impressed him with his knowledge of the new wet-plate photographic process. In any event, when Gardner arrived in America in 1856 to find that his Iowa settlement had been wiped out by "galloping consumption," he went to New York, where Brady promptly hired him. Gardner's resumé was impressive: he was familiar with the latest advances in photography, had excellent business instincts, and was educated in physics and chemistry, a valuable background for understanding the transfer of a live image onto a piece of paper.

Although they were both accomplished photographers, Brady and Gardner contrasted in many ways. Where Brady was a smooth talker and flamboyant in his lifestyle, Gardner was more intellectual and reserved. Brady cared little for record keeping. Gardner was meticulous about it. Brady delighted in preserving his own image in photographs, Gardner rarely stepped before the camera. In spite of these differences it seems they got along well. The Scot had found work with the most prestigious photographer in America, and Brady had come across a dependable, multi-talented employee. Brady dearly wanted to establish a gallery in the nation's capital, where stiff competition had shut down an earlier attempt. Recognizing Gardner's abilities, he took the plunge again in 1858, this time with Gardner as manager.

Gardner ran the Washington gallery differently than his employer would have. He standardized price schedules, hired a full-time bookkeeper, paid employees well, and allowed his photographers to accept free-lance offers in exchange for the resulting negatives. As civil war drew near, he anticipated demand for soldiers' portraits and arranged to have them mass-produced. Before long, the successful branch gallery was helping to support Brady's less profitable main location in New York.

A nation embroiled in civil war offered photographers a windfall of dramatic subjects, especially battlefield scenes that would take on historic value. Although both Brady and Gardner later claimed to have "conceived the idea of furnishing . . . a consecutive Photographic History" of the Civil War, in the early stages they each played different, yet significant roles in creating that record—Brady as financier, Gardner as field photographer. By late 1862, however, Brady's refusal to credit war photographs to Gardner (and other photographers who were imperiling their lives to enhance Brady's reputation) caused a growing rift between the two men.

In his New York gallery in October of 1862, Brady exhibited photographs of war dead from the battle of Antietam. The reaction was nothing short of sensational. Brady, the great photographer, had once again demonstrated his skills by becoming the first to record the "hideous orgy" of battlefield death with his camera. He accepted the accolades and surely enjoyed the attention, but it was all a charade—Brady had never been there. Every one of the photographs depicting the cruelties of war at Antietam was taken by Alexander Gardner, yet Brady could not bring himself to point this out to the public.

By spring of 1863, Gardner had had enough. He opened his own Washington gallery right around the corner from his former

Alexander Gardner's "Last Lincoln," perhaps the most valuable American photograph ever taken. Credit: National Portrait Gallery

employer and hired away a host of Brady's finest photographers. From this point on, the best "photographic history" of the Civil War was produced by Alexander Gardner and his men. Also, each print made by the Gardner gallery bore the name of the man responsible for both negative and positive images.

In addition to recording the Antietam bloodbath, which began a ghastly trend of death studies by many photographers that lasted until the end of the war, Gardner photographed Abraham Lincoln when the President came to Antietam two weeks after the battle. He also covered the hills and fields of

Gettysburg hardly hours after the gunfire had ceased, again concentating on scenes of intense combat and the resulting carnage. With captions stressing the heartbreak of wasted young lives, Gardner hoped to create a feeling of revulsion against war in all who saw the battle views.

On April 10, 1865, the day after Lee's surrender at Appomattox, Lincoln came to Gardner's studio for a series of portraits. He was an exhausted but relieved president—the Union was intact. For the last shot of the sitting, Gardner took a close-up bust of Lincoln. The face we see in that photograph reveals the staggering effect of four years of civil war. Horace Greeley described it as "haggard with care and seamed with thought and trouble. It looked care-ploughed, tempest-tossed, and weatherbeaten." Gardner made only one print of that final shot of the day before the negative broke and had to be discarded. It was to be the last photograph ever taken of Lincoln. Five days later he was dead.

Gardner gradually reduced his photographic activites following the war, although he illustrated a book of Robert Burns's poetry, financed a photographic expedition to Peru, and took a number of photographs of the West for the Union Pacific Railroad. A man of many talents, Gardner had invested wisely in real estate during his first decade in America, and consequently lived very comfortably in the post-war years. He eventually returned to his earlier interests in social welfare, but in a different form: life insurance. At the time of his death in 1882, he was president of a company that provided life insurance with premiums based on "the plan of issuing an assessment upon our members when a death occurs amongst them, and only then."

Alexander Gardner had a talent for capturing some of the most compelling images of the Civil War. He was never as famous as Mathew Brady, but it seems reasonable to assume that his interest in personal celebrity was secondary to his hopes of producing a valuable historical record. Perhaps his lack of self-promotion is the major reason Gardner remains in the shadows of Civil War history—his photographs certainly are a centerpiece.

Suggested Reading:

William A. Frassanito: *Antietam: The Photographic Legacy of America's Bloodiest Day* and *Gettysburg: A Journey in Time*

The Gerry-mander.

☞ *A* new species of *Monster*, which appeared in *Essex South District* in January la~~~

The original gerrymander. Note the hook-nosed profile on its backside. Descendants of this beast have been known to appear wherever politics is played. Credit: Library of Congress

Elbridge Gerry

Patriot, Statesman

b. July 17, 1744 Marblehead, Massachusetts
d. November 23, 1814 Washington, D.C.
Congressional

It is the duty of every man, though he may have but one day to live, to devote that day to the good of his country.

Elbridge Gerry

After narrowly losing a hard-fought legislative battle in the fledgling U.S. Congress, Thomas Jefferson summed up his frustration in three words: "Gerry changed sides." The remark is as good an epitaph as any for Elbridge Gerry, a devoted American patriot in his heart, but a confused and unpredictable thinker when it came to practical democracy. Gerry sailed with the tides of revolution and signed the Declaration of Independence, but could never decide what to do when it came to charting the course of the new nation's government. And although he eventually held the second highest office in the land, Gerry will be remembered primarily for the one word he contributed to our language: gerrymander.

Gerry joined his father's shipping and trading business in Boston after graduating from Harvard in 1762. By the early 1770s he had become staunchly anti-British, speaking out against crown control of the courts and unfair taxation. Six months before the Boston Tea Party, he advocated a boycott of British products.

Gerry's knowledge of shipping became invaluable as the colonies inched toward rebellion. He brought into Massachusetts a wide range of stores—everything from soap to gunpowder—that was secretly stockpiled for use by the minuteman militia. To prevent the British from seizing the stores in a surprise raid, on April 18, 1775, Gerry, John Hancock, Samuel Adams, and others met at a tavern located between Lexington and Concord and drew up plans for redistributing them.

After the meeting, Hancock and Adams left for home in Lexington, while Gerry took a room at the inn. Late that night, Hancock and Adams were saved by the famous ride of Paul Revere, but Gerry was awakened by the sound of troops marching toward the tavern. At first, the half-dressed Gerry wanted to challenge the soldiers at the front door, but on the tavern-keeper's advice he bolted out the back into the cold, moonlit night. Stumbling to the ground, he lay shivering in the shadows of corn stalks until the British had searched the inn and departed.

The zenith of Gerry's personal and public life was the signing of the colonies' Declaration of Independence in 1776. He worked hard to persuade others to sign it, prompting John Adams to say, "He is a man of immense worth. If every man here was a Gerry, the liberties of America would be safe against the gates of earth and hell." Few people in history are ever presented with the opportunity of creating a new nation, and Gerry was full of the idealism that accompanied such an act. So full, in fact, that he refused to sign the Constitution on grounds that it did not include enough safeguards to insure the survival of the new republic. Nonetheless, after the Constitution was ratified without him, he claimed a seat in the Congress.

As a statesman, Gerry found himself in a dilemma that his pursuit of independence had not resolved. In his gut he felt that some people were born to rule while others were not; his belief in democracy did not extend so far as to include the riffraff. Unable to reconcile within himself what to do about it, he constantly vascillated from side to side on issues, sometimes even rejecting his own proposals when it came time to vote. He was at various times an independent, a Federalist, and a Republican, guided only by a starry notion that real statesman-patriots transcend partisan politics to consider the national welfare above all. Near the end of his life he had reversed himself on that idea, too, and was a constant source of exasperation to leaders who counted on his support.

In 1797, President Adams sent Gerry, John Marshall, and Charles C. Pinckney to France to negotiate lingering disputes between the two nations. In Paris, French foreign minister Talleyrand sent undercover agents, code-named X, Y, and Z, to demand bribes before serious talks got under way. Marshall and Pinckney left in disgust, but Gerry stayed on against Adams's orders, believing his departure would lead to war. Finally, Adams sent a ship to bring Gerry back, and for years after Gerry was criticized for his disobedient behavior in the XYZ affair.

In 1810, Gerry was elected to the first of two one-year terms as governor of Massachusetts. His first term was noteworthy for its moderation. But by the second term, Gerry had abandoned any pretense of noble statesmanship, engaging in extremes of partisan politics. Gerry and the Republicans controlled the state legislature and moved to secure their majority by chopping up voting districts, lumping all Federal strongholds into a few districts while maintaining comfortable Republican majorities in most of the state. One of the new districts was so absurdly long and contorted that it was said to resemble a salamander. Salamander quickly became "Gerry-mander" in honor of the governor, and the word soon took its place in the language, denoting any rearrangement of voting districts that favors one party over another. In a cartoon drawing of the original gerrymandered district, the ugly animal's backside reveals a very unflattering profile intended to be Elbridge Gerry's face. And in the next election, in spite of all the district manipulations, Gerry was run out of office.

Now unemployed and deep in debt, Gerry wrote President Madison, practically begging for a job. What he got was the nomination for vice-president, based on his strong support for Madison's 1812 pro-war stand. Gerry's New England background helped balance Madison's Virginia roots, and the ticket won the election, putting the mixed-up Gerry only a heartbeat away from the White House.

On November 23, 1814, while riding in his carriage to take his seat as president of the Senate, Vice-President Elbridge Gerry suddenly became sick. He died within 20 minutes, but not before giving us all a word that describes a uniquely political reptile.

Suggested Reading:

George Athan Billias: *Elbridge Gerry: Founding Father and Republican Statesman*

Dashiell Hammett

Mystery Writer

b. May 27, 1894 St. Mary's County, Maryland
d. January 10, 1961 New York, New York
Arlington

Samuel D. Hammett is a mystery; few people
even recognize his name on the simple headstone. But just
mention *The Maltese Falcon* and *The Thin Man*, two classics of
detective fiction, and the mystery seems solved. With books
like these, Hammett took murder out of the parlor and into the
street. Witty, tough, and unsentimental, reflecting the abandon
and desperation of the Depression, his hardboiled writing style
was new and immensely popular. It brought the detective novel
to the level of art.

His skill and popularity, however, tell us little about Dashiell
Hammett, the man. At one time president of the Writer's
League of America and an outspoken political activist, Hammett virtually stopped writing at age 39 and lived his last years
in seclusion in Katonah, New York, where three typewriters
gathered dust in his cottage. During an interview in 1957,
Hammett called himself a "two-fisted loafer" and claimed he
kept the typewriters to remind him that he had once been a
writer.

Born near Lexington Park, Maryland, and educated in Baltimore, Dashiell Hammett became a Pinkerton detective when
just 21. After winning promotion for catching a man who had
stolen a ferris wheel, he spent roughly seven years living the
life he described so well in his books. "I was a detective,"
Hammett later said, "so I wrote about detectives. Everything
came from that."

Being a detective had its bizarre moments. On one occasion
the police gave Hammett a detailed description of a suspect
complete even to the mole on his neck, but failed to mention
the man had only one arm. On another job, the detective spent
several months as a hospital patient shadowing a man in the
adjoining bed.

In 1928, Knopf publishers received the manuscript of a

book entitled *Poinsonville* along with a letter claiming the author planned to change the face of detective writing. Four novels and six years later, the public agreed that Dashiell Hammett had done just that.

"When a man's partner is killed he's supposed to do something about it," says Sam Spade after his friend, Miles Archer, is gunned down in a San Francisco alley. What Spade does about it fills the pages of *The Maltese Falcon* (1930), Hammett's finest novel and the prototype of a genre. Dealing with the theft of a jewel-encrusted statue of a falcon, the book is a tour-de-force not because of its raw violence, but because of its suspense. Although guns are drawn and threats are made, bullets and blood never dominate. "The essence of suspense," Hammett once declared, "is that while it lasts nothing happens." Even at the climax, when the bird is retrieved, we get tight, crackling dialogue instead of a shootout.

Did the Maltese Falcon really exist? No. But the inspiration for the treasure apparently came from a real jeweled skull of a Tibetan monk smuggled out of India and owned by one of Hammett's friends.

The Thin Man, Hammett's next big book, appeared in 1934. To write it the author holed up in New York's Sutton Hotel, working 30 hours at a stretch, chain smoking, and drinking endless cups of coffee to stay awake. The hotel's night manager, Nathanael West—also a struggling writer—arranged for Hammett's free room and board. On the surface *The Thin Man* lacks the intensity of *The Maltese Falcon*, but the subtle humor and the addition of a strong female character made it an overnight best-seller.

Hammett's tough-talking hard-hitting private eyes reached millions of people not alone through the machine-gun paced tales, but also through comic strips and films. Capitalizing on the success of *Dick Tracy*, which had appeared three years earlier, Hammett started his own detective comic strip in 1934, *Secret Agent X-9*. Written by Hammett and drawn by Alex Raymond, creator of *Flash Gordon*, the strip followed the violent adventures of "X-9," a mysterious, nameless crime fighter. The author filled the strip with the same hard characters found in his novels but he added a powerful dose of action. X-9 carries a gun and he uses it, in one episode killing four men in four panels.

When Hammett's stories were transferred to the screen, the leading parts attracted some of the biggest names in Holly-

Dashiell Hammett's short-lived comic strip, Secret Agent X-9. Credit: Library of Congress

wood. The role of Sam Spade in *The Maltese Falcon* seemed tailor-made for the cynical Humphrey Bogart, and the sophisticated eroticism of William Powell and Myrna Loy in *The Thin Man* was popular enough to inspire a string of successful sequels.

Strangely, just as the big contracts rolled in, Hammett turned from writing to politics. Partly due to the influence of the playwright Lillian Hellman, his confidant and lover, Hammett now dedicated himself to radical causes. With Ernest Hemingway and John Dos Passos, he fervently supported the leftists fighting the Spanish Civil War. His appearance at Marxist rallies sparked the FBI to start a file on Hammett; the former detective now was under surveillance for days at a time.

When World War II broke out, Hammett was anxious to enlist against Fascism. The Army, suspicious of the motives that would send an overaged, underweight novelist to a recruiting center, accepted him but shipped him to the Aleutians, eight hundred miles off the coast of Alaska. There, on the barren island of Adak, Hammett edited the military newspaper and studied the northern lights.

Hammett returned from the war a quieter, more solitary man. The United States had changed too. The time was ripe for a new wave and, led by Senator Joseph McCarthy, it took shape as an anti-communist scare. In 1951, the author was subpoenaed by a federal court to answer questions about his political activities. Knowing full well the consequences of failure to cooperate, Hammett nevertheless pleaded the fifth amendment and was summarily sentenced to six months in prison. He told Hellman, "If it were more than jail, if it were my life, I would give it for what I think democracy is, and I don't let cops or judges tell me what I think democracy is."

Already suffering from bad health, the author emerged from prison a broken 57-year-old man. His books out of print, his money spent, Hammett retired to Katonah to collect a small government pension.

When he died in 1961, Dashiell Hammett was buried in Arlington National Cemetery according to his wishes. The FBI closed its 278-page file on Hammett noting "the incongruous situation which exists wherein one who has been a member of an organization which believes in the overthrow of our government by force and violence receives a hero's burial among those who gave their lives to support this government." Having volunteered for duty in two world wars, and having won several medals and commendations, Hammett had earned his honored resting place.

Hardboiled Hammett

Samuel Spade's jaw was long and bony, his chin a jutting V under the more flexible V of his mouth. His nostrils curved back to make another, smaller, V. His yellow-grey eyes were horizontal. The V motif was picked up again by thickish brows rising outward from twin creases above a hooked nose, and his pale brown hair grew down—from high flat temples—in a point on his forehead. He looked rather like a blond Satan. He said to Effie Perine: "Yes, sweetheart?"

opening of The Maltese Falcon (1930)

A telephone-bell rang in the darkness. When it had rung three times bed-springs creaked, fingers fumbled on wood, something small and hard thudded on a carpeted floor, the springs creaked again, and a man's voice said: "Hello. . . Yes, speaking . . . Dead?. . . 15 minutes. Thanks."

The Maltese Falcon

Babe liked Sue. Vassos liked Sue. Sue liked Babe. Babe didn't like that.

"Fly Paper" (1929)

The Filipino turned around, looked at me, ducking his head sharply, and bolted for the street. The three who were left shot their drinks down their gullets and tried to catch my eye. I was reading a sign high on the wall behind the bar:

ONLY GENUINE PRE-WAR AMERICAN AND
BRITISH WHISKEYS SERVED HERE

I was trying to count how many lies could be found in those nine words, and had reached four, with the promise of more when one of my confederates, the Greek, cleared his throat with the noise of a gasoline engine's backfire. Goose-neck was edging down the bar, a bung-starter in one hand, his face purple.

"The Golden Horseshoe"

Suggested Reading:

William E. Nolan: *Hammett: A Life at the Edge*
Diane Johnson: *Dashiell Hammett: A Life*

Oliver Wendell Holmes, Jr.

Jurist

b. March 8, 1841 Boston, Massachusetts
d. March 5, 1935 Washington, D.C.
Arlington

Judges usually live in a serene obscurity, painstakingly applying rules of law to the way we live. Headlines go
to the law makers and breakers while back pages briefly note
the rulings of the courts. Oliver Wendell Holmes, Jr., Associ-
ate Justice of the United States Supreme Court, wasn't exactly
a front page celebrity, but he is probably the best known justice in American history. As "the founder of modern jurispru-
dence," he launched a new interpretation of law based on a
simple theory: people change, so law must change with them.
Along the way, he survived three Civil War battle wounds,
called Abraham Lincoln a fool, took in a few burlesque shows,
and left us with a wonderful assortment of stories, humor, and
wisdom for living.

A native of Boston, Holmes was the son of writer and physi-
cian Oliver Wendell Holmes, the "autocrat of the breakfast
table" and author of the poem "Old Ironsides." In the intellectual and cultural swirl that was pre-Civil War Boston, young
Holmes was exposed to his father's friends, among them Ralph
Waldo Emerson, Henry Wadsworth Longfellow, and Nathaniel
Hawthorne.

Shortly before his graduation from Harvard in 1861, Holmes
was commissioned a lieutenant in the 20th Massachusetts Volunteers, a regiment which would rank among the highest in
war casualties for the North. At Ball's Bluff, on the Potomac
River near Leesburg, Virginia, Holmes was hit in the gut by a
spent musket ball and fell, momentarily stunned. Ashamed to
withdraw from the fight with so little excuse as a bruised belly,
Holmes got up and charged ahead, waving his sword and
cheering his comrades on. Within moments, a second ball went
through his chest. Fortunate to have escaped instant death,
Holmes was luckier still to be carried down the cliffside and
ferried across the river to safety amid the chaos of drowning

Oliver Wendell Holmes, Jr. Credit: Library of Congress

men and enemy fire. Later, Holmes wrote down as much of this "novel" experience as he could remember, and noted that "one of the thoughts that made it seem particularly hard to die was the recollection of several fair damsels whom I wasn't quite ready to leave."

Holmes recalled that at Antietam, on the bloodiest day in American history, "Troops came along our flank and someone said, 'Don't shoot, they are our men.' Well, they weren't, and I got a bullet in the back of the neck. I thought I was a gone coon." Miraculously, Holmes survived the wound. At Chancellorsville, a piece of shrapnel ripped into his heel. After recovering for a third time, he was relieved of any more battle duty and sent to man the defenses around Washington, D.C.

In July 1864, General Jubal Early's rebel forces were encamped near the Capital, and President Lincoln wanted to see them. Holmes was chosen as the President's escort and took him to a fort where he might glimpse the enemy. Seemingly unaware of any danger, the tall Lincoln, with his big stove-pipe hat, stood straight up to have a look. Immediately, Confederate bullets started flying and Holmes yanked the President behind the earthworks shouting "Get down, you fool!" Astonished that he could ever have addressed the President so improperly, Holmes breathed easier when Lincoln later told him, "I'm glad to see you know how to talk to a civilian."

The war over, Holmes earned his law degree from Harvard in 1866 and soon plunged himself into an exhaustive study of legal history and practice. He was amazed to find that courts still followed age-old laws without questioning their relevance to modern times. "It is revolting to have no better reason for a rule of law than that it was laid down in the time of Henry IV," he wrote. "It is still more revolting if the grounds upon which it was laid down have vanished long since, and the rule simply persists from blind imitation of the past." In 1881 Holmes published his opinions in *The Common Law*, a book that changed legal thinking on both sides of the Atlantic and revealed Holmes's talent for simplifying legal gobbledygook. He distilled the essence of common law into one sentence: "The life of the law has not been logic, it has been experience." He argued that law was not a sacred, rigid formula; it was as fluid as civilization and must always be changed to keep up. *The Common Law* was then, and still is, considered a classic of legal thought.

A year after the publication of his book, Holmes, only 41, was appointed to the Massachusetts Supreme Court, and in 1899 he became its Chief Justice. In 1902 President Roosevelt appointed him to the United States Supreme Court, where he served for 29 years. He became known as the "Great Dissenter," not because he frequently differed with the majority— he dissented in only one of every ten decisions—but because his dissents often presaged eventual changes in the law.

In 1872, Holmes married Fanny Bowditch Dixwell, the daughter of the tutor who had prepared him for Harvard. It is said that Fanny loved the thrill of firemen battling a blaze, and whenever a clanging fire engine passed by, she'd holler, "Come on, Wendell, let's go!" and the Supreme Court Justice would run off hand in hand with his wife after the firefighters. After her death in 1929, Holmes was noticeably less gay-spirited.

From time to time, Justice Holmes raised a few staid eyebrows by taking in a burlesque show. Once, during a truly eye-popping performance, he turned to a companion and said, "Thank God I am a man of low tastes." Devouring sometimes more than a hundred books per year, Holmes enjoyed reading Greek and Roman classics in translation, but preferred "the purple passages in the original." His advice to boring, long-winded attorneys was to read some "naughty French novels." Known to spice his private conversation with an occasional profanity, Holmes observed, "You will never appreciate the potentialities of the English language until you have heard a Southern mule driver search the soul of a mule."

Even from the highest court in the land Holmes found time for a humorous aside. A fellow justice, William R. Day, was a little, frail man. His son, tall and robust, once argued a case before the court, doing an excellent job of it. Holmes scribbled a note and passed it along the bench: "A block off the old chip."

The Supreme Court Justice with the bushy-winged moustache carried in him more than a sense of humor. He was constantly reminded of the value of life by the scars of his battle wounds and he appreciated the lessons the war had taught him early in life. "Through our great good fortune," he told a group of veterans in 1884, "in our youth our hearts were touched with fire." That fire burned in Holmes throughout his nearly 94 years. He was almost 90 when he absorbed himself in a copy of Thucydides in the original Greek. Why tackle such a work at such a late age? "Because," he said, "no gentleman should go to his grave without first having read Thucydides in the original."

Below are some memorable sayings of Oliver Wendell Holmes, Jr. A number of them were first applied to the law, but they can easily be related to daily life:

Every calling is great when greatly pursued.

I think that, as life is action and passion, it is required of a man that he should share the passion and action of his time at peril of being judged not to have lived.

A dog will fight for his bone.

The most far-reaching form of power is not money; it is the command of ideas.

A man cannot shift his misfortunes to his neighbor's shoulders.

The great act of faith is when man decides that he is not God.

Life is an end in itself, and the only question as to whether it is worth living is whether you have had enough of it.

Life is painting a picture, not doing a sum.

The man of action has the present, but the thinker controls the future.

Taxes are what we pay for a civilized society.
(Carved into the frieze of the IRS building in Washington, D.C.)

Suggested Reading:

Mark DeWolfe Howe: *Justice Oliver Wendell Holmes: The Shaping Years, 1841–1870*
E. P. Meyer: *That Remarkable Man: Justice Oliver Wendell Holmes*
Julius J. Mark: *The Holmes Reader*

J. Edgar Hoover

FBI Director

b. January 1, 1895 Washington, D.C.
d. May 2, 1972 Washington, D.C.
Congressional

"**D**on't shoot, G-men! Don't shoot!"
Kidnapper "Machine Gun" Kelly cowered in a corner when
the FBI had him trapped; he whimpered and pleaded for his
life. His wife was so disgusted with his un-gangster-like behavior she called him a rat. "You've disgraced my family," she told
him. Unlike Bonnie and Clyde, John Dillinger, and Ma Barker,
who were all gunned down in shootouts worthy of Hollywood,
Kelly turned yellow, put up his hands, and surrendered. A
shameful act in the eyes of his wife, maybe, but a wise move
considering the fate of others who attempted to shoot their way
past the FBI. And in giving up, Kelly had coined what became
the nation's favorite nickname for FBI agents: "G-men."

The G-men, or Government Men, were the highly educated,
thoroughly trained lawmen who for nearly 50 years mirrored
the style and character of the first FBI director, J. Edgar
Hoover.

John Edgar Hoover was well suited to his life's work. Although a line drive baseball had given him a classic gangster's
nose as a teen, he was anything but an outlaw. His mother,
with whom he lived until her death, instilled in him a rigid
sense of discipline and moral values. As a young Justice Department lawyer, he had built a reputation as a sharp, hardworking patriot and a stickler for detail. When Attorney General Harlan F. Stone was looking for someone to take over the
graft-ridden Bureau of Investigation in 1924, he found the right
man in 29-year-old J. Edgar Hoover.

Hoover's appointment marked the birth of the Federal Bureau
of Investigation, although it didn't get that name until 1935.
The new director concentrated on clearing out the corruption
and fashioning a law enforcement team comparable to Scotland
Yard. He hired only clean-cut lawyers and accountants as
agents, personally approving each one, and established a train-

ing academy at Quantico, Virginia. Embracing a new, "thinking man's" approach to law enforcement, Hoover also set up a scientific crime laboratory and a fingerprint library (now containing over two hundred million entries). Within ten years, the FBI had become the most efficient crime-fighting machine in the world.

It was in the 1930s that Hoover and the FBI captured the imagination of a nation that had had little to cheer about during the Depression. An epidemic of kidnapping for ransom was made "virtually extinct" by the Bureau's relentless pursuit, and gangsters like "Baby Face" Nelson and "Pretty Boy" Floyd, who had killed FBI agents, were cornered and killed in highly publicized gun battles. During these years of gangster shootouts and sensational headlines, Hoover used the media to make himself a national hero. He orchestrated a flood of FBI books, movies, comics, and other publicity, while his columnist friend Walter Winchell constantly lauded the director's successes. Young boys joined "junior G-man" clubs and manufacturers turned out an array of G-man toys, games, and clothes. Hoover's "ten most wanted" list found a prominent place in the nation's post offices, and changes in the list kept the public abreast of the FBI's latest captures. Irritated by the extensive publicity given some criminals, Hoover defended his own showboating by declaring, "If there's going to be publicity, let it be on the side of law and order."

Shortly before the second World War, President Roosevelt extended Hoover's responsibilities into the spy-catching business. The most notable case involved the capture of 33 Nazi spies in 1941. To gather evidence against the spies, a bugged office was set up with a two-way mirror. An FBI man posed as a Nazi contact and easily got the spies to reveal their secrets while a movie camera recorded everything through the mirror. In another case, eight would-be saboteurs were caught when one of them squealed, certain that the G-men were on his trail. Actually, the FBI had not yet tracked down the saboteur, but the Bureau's reputation for getting its man was so strong that he panicked and turned himself in.

Hoover used the FBI to gather information on suspected communists during the McCarthy era, and was instrumental in gaining the conviction of Julius and Ethel Rosenberg for passing atomic secrets to the Soviets. In 1958, he published his detailed condemnation of communism, *Masters of Deceit*, which sold 2½ million copies. But while Hoover immersed himself in

Never one to shy away from publicity, J. Edgar Hoover frequently mingled with famous personalities. Here he meets Marilyn Monroe at the Waldorf-Astoria Hotel in New York. The fellow in the middle is Milton Berle.

Credit: National Archives.

ferreting out communists, other groups were allowed to flourish. The Ku Klux Klan lynched countless blacks without fear of FBI pursuit, and Hoover refused to believe in the existence of the Mafia until shortly before his death.

Hoover's access to information about all sorts of people gave him a unique power in the federal government. The FBI had over 1500 files on members of Congress, and when necessary for his purposes, Hoover used compromising information to intimidate them. The Justice Department reported in the 1960s that "the control and management of J. Edgar Hoover" was any

Attorney General's "greatest single problem." Although he was answerable to the Attorney General, Hoover resented any and all attempts to bridle him. His most publicized clashes were with Robert F. Kennedy, who enforced his authority over the FBI and its director. On November 22, 1963, Hoover callously informed Bobby of President Kennedy's assassination. According to RFK, Hoover sounded "not quite as excited as if he were reporting the fact that he had found a communist on the faculty of Howard University." The two men never spoke again.

Although Hoover remained a bachelor all his life, it was often said that he was married—to the FBI. His closest friend was Clyde Tolson, his assistant director. They ate lunch and dinner together for over 40 years and were familiar faces at Washington area race tracks. Hoover was always an avid walker, and his morning walks with Tolson became famous for their punctual regularity. Hoover's next closest companions were his dogs, and he provided in his will for those that survived him. One of his first dogs was named "Spee Dee Bozo" and he had several named "G-boy."

Author Tom Wicker wrote that J. Edgar Hoover "wielded more power, longer, than any man in American history." In simpler days, when Hoover's FBI was out chasing kidnappers and gangsters, he was a national idol. In more complex times, when the bad guys were harder to distinguish, Hoover's methods came under heavy criticism. He was accused of tapping the phones of congressmen and attempted (with much success) to silence his critics by leaking incriminating intelligence about them to the press. His reputation has been tarnished ever since. But Hoover's contributions to law enforcement have been copied throughout the world and there is no doubt that he dedicated his life to the good of his country.

Suggested Reading:

Ovid Demaris: *The Director*
Sanford J. Ungar: *The FBI*

A cartoon of Robert Ingersoll, the "Illustrious Infidel." Credit: Library of Congress

Robert Ingersoll

Orator, Agnostic

> b. August 11, 1833 Dresden, New York
> d. July 21, 1899 Dobbs Ferry, New York
> Arlington

Robert Green Ingersoll. Enemies dubbed him "Robert Godless Injuresoul," and "the devil's dynamo." Friends called him "Matchless Bob," a "prophet" sent to save the human race. He was the most openly denounced, secretly admired man in the country; and everyone agreed on one thing: he was controversial.

One hundred years ago, Robert Ingersoll was as well known as Abraham Lincoln. In the struggle between religion and science sparked by Charles Darwin, Ingersoll used his brilliant speaking ability to lambast orthodox beliefs and spread the gospel of humanism. During the closing decades of the 19th century, he was the premier orator of the nation.

The son of an Illinois minister, Ingersoll received his education in the basement of a Congregational church. He read and rejected the Bible at an early age but was inspired and moved by William Shakespeare and Robert Burns. Years later, when asked if he kept a Bible, Ingersoll produced a beautifully bound volume of Shakespeare with blank pages for recording births and marriages. "This," he declared solemnly, "is our family Bible." Opening a volume of Burns he added, "and this is our Prayer Book."

In 1854, Ingersoll was admitted to the Illinois bar and soon had a thriving practice in Peoria. His natural gift for persuasive oratory made him a popular trial lawyer. Although he practiced law for the rest of his life, he often criticized the profession, and once wrote his brother: "We have a very nice office and lighted with gas. Gas you know is an excellent thing in law, in fact indispensable."

During the Civil War, Ingersoll entered the Union cavalry as a colonel. At the battle of Corinth he was captured by General Forrest and entertained the Confederates with his verbal wizardry. One story depicts him delivering an eloquent anti-slavery speech to his cheering captors. Fearing the desertion of his troops to the Yankee colonel, Forrest declared he would gladly trade Ingersoll for a Union mule. After what Ingersoll termed a "brief and jovial season of captivity," he was released and returned home.

Ingersoll first received national attention at the 1876 Republican convention where he delivered a flamboyant speech nominating James G. Blaine for president. It is sometimes called the greatest nominating speech in American history. Ingersoll brought the delegates to their feet with this magnificent bombast:

Like an armed warrior, like a plumed knight, James G. Blaine marched down the halls of the American Congress and threw his shining lance full and fair against the brazen foreheads of the defamers of his country and the maligners of its honor. For the Republican Party to desert this gallant leader now, is as though an army should desert their general upon the field of battle!

Although Blaine lost the nomination, Ingersoll had so many requests for his services that he hired a full-time clerk to answer his mail.

Following the convention, Ingersoll made a triumphant transcontinental lecture tour. Speaking on religion—his favorite topic—he inflamed, amused, and educated the capacity crowds. In lectures with titles like "Some Mistakes of Moses," and "Why I am an Agnostic," he denounced the old creeds and spread the new:

Is there an intelligent man or woman now in the world who believes the Garden of Eden story? If you find any man who believes it, strike his forehead and you will hear an echo. Something is for rent.

I believe in Observation, Reason and Experience—the Blessed Trinity of Science. I believe in Man, Woman and Child—the Blessed Trinity of Love and Joy.

His wit was sharp and he peppered his lectures with quotable one-liners: "With soap, baptism is a good thing." "An honest God is the noblest work of Man."

The clergy called him a "moral leper," and charged him with "peddling infidelity at $500 a night." But their protests were Ingersoll's best advertisement. The louder they complained, the larger his audiences grew. Walt Whitman saw him and stated, Ingersoll "runs on like a stream: is sweet, fluid—like precious ointment."

While lecturing in the West, Ingersoll met Lew Wallace, the author, on a train to Indianapolis. "The Great Agnostic" was in fine fettle and held Wallace spellbound for several hours with his pungent critique of Christianity. Wallace was so affected that, as he later said, he wrote his great Christian novel, *Ben Hur: A Tale of the Christ*, as a reply to Ingersoll's skepticism.

If Ingersoll wasn't a Christian, he did have faith in humanity:

Humanity is the grand religion, and no God can put a man in hell in another world who has made a little heaven in this. God cannot make a man miserable if that man has made somebody else happy. God cannot hate anybody who is capable of loving anybody. Humanity—that word embraces all there is.

He valued the family above all else and visitors considered his household a model of paradise. "You are my Gods, and I worship you," he told his wife and daughters.

A champion of women's rights and racial equality, Ingersoll welcomed Susan B. Anthony when she came to Illinois and used his verbal skill to defend her from hecklers. When Frederick Douglass was turned away from every hotel in Peoria, Ingersoll opened his home to him. Douglass, deeply religious, concluded that being an infidel was no more a sign of wickedness than being orthodox was a sign of honesty.

Ingersoll's critics predicted that when he died he would be begging God's forgiveness, and claimed he carried an emergency statement refuting his beliefs, to be read in case he died suddenly. Ingersoll did die suddenly, but peacefully. There was no statement revealed, no deathbed conversion, but widespread grief. Mark Twain wrote, "except for my daughter's, I have not grieved for any death as I have grieved for his. His was a great and beautiful spirit, he was a man—all man from his crown to his foot soles."

The Gospel According to Ingersoll

Many people think they have religion when they are merely troubled with dyspepsia.

"Thou shalt not kill" is as old as life itself. And for this reason a large majority of people in all countries have objected to being murdered.

Drunkenness is one form of intemperance, prohibition is another.

The men who declare that woman is the intellectual inferior of man, do not and cannot, by offering themselves in evidence, substantiate their declaration.

Each nation has created a god, and the god has always resembled his creators. He hated and loved what they hated and loved, and he was invariably found on the side of those in power. Each god was intensely patriotic, and detested all nations but his own.

I do not consider it a very important question whether Christ was the Son of God or not. After all, what difference does it make? If he never existed, we are under the same obligation to do what we believe is right; and believing that he was the Son of God or disbelieving it is of no earthly importance. If we are ever judged at all it will be by our actions, and not our beliefs.

A good deed is the best prayer; a loving life is the best religion.

Do not most people mistake for freedom the right to examine their own chains?

Suggested Reading:

C. H. Cramer: *Royal Bob, the Life of Robert G. Ingersoll*
David D. Anderson: *Robert Ingrsoll*

Adelaide Johnson

Feminist, Sculptor

b. September 26, 1859 Plymouth, Illinois
d. November 10, 1955 Washington, D.C.
Congressional

In 1875, 16-year-old Sarah Adeline Johnson, an art student in St. Louis, Missouri, noted wryly that the term "Pilgrim Fathers" made no mention of Pilgrim mothers. It was bold thinking for a midwestern teenager 45 years before women got the vote, but Sarah, who later changed her name to Adelaide, was not one to conform to traditional attitudes, especially when the subject was equality of the sexes. As an adult, she combined her dedication to the rights of women with her talent as a sculptor to become the "Sculptor of the Woman Movement," preserving in marble the notable figures of early feminism. Her largest work, the sculpture of Lucretia Mott, Elizabeth Cady Stanton, and Susan B. Anthony which stands in the U.S. Capitol, is the only national monument to the women's movement.

As a young woman, Johnson displayed enough natural artistic ability that in 1884 Giulio Monteverde, a revered Italian sculptor, took her on as his only student. She studied with him in Rome for 11 years. In 1886, Johnson met the founder of the women's movement, Susan B. Anthony, in Italy and began a long friendship with her that verged on idolatry. Within a year she had completed her first sculpture of Anthony, which was made a part of the permanent collection of the Metropolitan Museum of Art in New York. Setting a precedent, the museum acquired the piece while both artist and subject were still alive. Later, in 1936, the work was used as the model for a commemorative stamp of the feminist leader.

In 1896, Johnson married Alexander Jenkins, an English businessman, in her studio in Washington, D.C. In the progressive spirit of the women's movement, Johnson kept her own last name while Jenkins gave his up for hers. A little less progressive about revealing her true age, Johnson, who was 36, gave her age as 24 on the marriage certificate. That made her

Adelaide Johnson poses with her monument to the women's movement, depicting (l. to r.) Elizabeth Cady Stanton, Susan B. Anthony, and Lucretia Mott. Credit: Library of Congress

a comfortable one year younger than her new husband.

Johnson's choice to retain her own name in marriage seemed to be influenced by her relationship with Anthony, as noted in her description of the unique ceremony, which was performed by a woman priest:

*The guests all arrived in white and ignorant of the occasion until 9
o'clock (when the ceremony began). . . The two guests in marble on
either side were Elizabeth Cady Stanton and Susan B. Anthony, in
truth, my bridesmaids. . . Blessed Susan was herself there in form and
addressed us delightfully, saying it was the first occasion when a man
had done a thing so royal, so noble. . . She seemed to positively for-
give me for marrying at all because of this fact. . .*

By 1908, Mr. and Mrs. Johnson had drifted apart and were divorced. They had no children.

Johnson made busts of many well known people of her time,
among them the naturalist John Burroughs and the famous "po-
etess of passion," Ella Wheeler Wilcox (see John A. Joyce).
She also sculpted series of liberal religious thinkers and edu-
cators. But her life's work was centered on giving artistic and
historical significance to the women's movement through marble
portraits of its early leaders. In 1921, after 20 years' work,
Johnson's tremendous sculpture of Mott, Stanton, and Anthony
was presented to the nation and unveiled in the Capitol. At
more than seven tons, the work dwarfed the 97-pound woman
who created it. Although then an observer told Johnson that
her work brought out the "Woman in women," the severe, determined women in bonnets and shawls who emerge from the
mammoth base of the sculpture today appear old-fashioned and
nearly ferocious, which probably accounts for the statue's irrev-
erent nickname, "biddies in a bathtub."

On Susan B. Anthony's birthday in 1934, Johnson gave a
speech at the Capitol which she regarded as an emancipation
proclamation for women. She hailed "the awakening of woman"
as "the central and supreme fact in the world of today," and
observed that "the revolution embodied in the woman movement represents the potentiality, if not yet the dawn, of ethics
in the human race." She went on:

*This crusade was made with but one weapon—a righteous idea—the
right of the human unit to freedom. Suffrage, the struggle which was
so prolonged and made so spectacular by the opposition, was but one
item, and became impinged on the mass mind, but [it] will pass . . .
as the mightier thing 'Equal Rights' becomes established.*

In addition to having campaigned for women's right to vote,
Johnson also fought for a woman's right to smoke and to earn
money for herself, not for her husband.

Johnson's financial situation deteriorated during the 1930s.
In November 1939, at age 80, she was $12,000 in debt; her

heat had been turned off, and the phone company had sent a final demand for payment before discontinuing service. Forced to consider selling some of her sculpture, Johnson was outraged by the puny offers she received. Claiming that not even Rockefeller could afford her art, she clubbed to pieces many of her busts and clay studies and then called in the press to witness the destruction. The demonstration generated enough publicity that concerned individuals organized to pay off her debts.

In the mid-1940s, Johnson changed her age again. She added 12 years to her actual age and began celebrating well-publicized birthdays as an centenarian. In 1951, she won $500 on the television quiz show "Strike It Rich." Asked who had written "The Battle Hymn of The Republic," Johnson answered correctly "Julia Ward Howe." No wonder. Howe was well known to Johnson as an early suffragist.

A vegetarian since the 1880s, Johnson advised those seeking long life to avoid the poisons in meats. When she died in 1955, newspapers listed her age as 107 or 108, both wrong. She was really only 96, but that's not bad either.

Suggested Reading:

Edith Mayo: "Johnson, Alelaide;" Notable American Women: The Modern Period: Edited by Sicherman and Green

John A. Joyce

Poet

b. July 4, 1842 Shraugh, Ireland
d. January 18, 1915 Washington, D.C.
Oak Hill

These rocks of rhyme and pebbles of poetry I throw into the world of thought, trusting that they may macadamize the highway of life.

from preface to Joyce's Complete Poems (1900)

Shoulder-length white hair and a red bow tie, a blue frock coat and a wide-brimmed felt hat—those were his trademarks. Known throughout the country as a delightful eccentric, John Alexander Joyce was a self-proclaimed philosopher and an awful poet of the sincerely saccharine, sensitive sing-song sort (whew!) who limbered up an era stiffened by proper Victorian values. He is usually remembered in connection with a dispute over authorship of the famous lines

Laugh, and the world laughs with you;
Weep, and you weep alone.

But there was much more to him than that.

The son of Irish immigrants who came to America in 1846, Joyce was raised in West Virginia and Kentucky towns that thrived on commerce along the Ohio River. At 12 he became fed up with school and set out on his own. Like Mark Twain's later creation Huckleberry Finn, Joyce traveled the Ohio and Mississippi rivers by steamboat, part of the time as a pilot's apprentice.

In 1860, at 18, Joyce rented a hall in Pittsburgh and before an almost empty room expounded on his theory "of running things by perpetually acting balances suspended like a see-saw plank on a middle pivot throwing out living oil into the fibers of the great machine." Not long after, he was forcibly committed to the Kentucky State Asylum where he "made friends of

117

John A. Joyce is beside himself. Credit: Peter Exton

two little mice and a family of grey spiders." A fellow inmate was Theodore Clay, son of Henry Clay.

After two months in the asylum Joyce was released; and at the outbreak of the Civil War he joined the Union army, the only member of his family to side with the North. In the years after the war, Joyce was a teacher, a tax collector, and then a lawyer, making a career with the Internal Revenue. At one point, he was sent to the Pacific Coast to investigate complaints of collusion between revenue officers and whiskey distillers. His descriptions of the trip praise the splendors of life in the Far West, except when he sailed up the Columbia River:

The fur-bearing animals of this region have almost entirely disappeared, and the great havoc by voracious fishermen will soon destroy the grandest salmon fisheries on the continent. A law should be enacted to protect the fish of this stream from the wholesale slaughter that now goes on, in and out of season.

The year was 1874!

At St. Louis the next year, in a case steeped in political shadiness, Joyce himself was convicted of whiskey fraud. Furious at the verdict handed down by his political enemies, he was determined to enjoy himself in prison. He spent the entire two-year sentence in an unlocked cell performing many of the warden's duties, monitoring other prisoners, and writing lots of poetry. Heading straight for Washington after serving his term, Joyce personally requested and received a full pardon from President Rutherford B. Hayes.

Joyce probably published his first book of poems as a result of seeing someone else's name under his own poetry. Ella Wheeler Wilcox, a far more popular, but not much better, poet than Joyce, published "Solitude" in 1883. In it were the lines "Laugh, and the world laughs with you; weep, and you weep alone." Insisting that Wilcox had stolen the words from a poem he had written 20 years earlier, Joyce invited litigation to settle authorship and produced affidavits from old friends who had heard him recite the lines before Wilcox claimed to have written them. Although Joyce gained notoriety through the controversy, the matter was never resolved, except that historians uniformly credit the lines to Wilcox.

No doubt feeling burned, yet elated that his work was worth stealing, Joyce proceeded to publish voluminously. He recited with very little coaxing and became widely known as the "Poet of Washington." He loved long strings of alliteration, mauled meter mercilessly, and generally stuck to two seemingly conflicting themes: (1) hard work and virtue will make you rich and powerful; (2) the rich and powerful are inherently rotten.

When not philosophizing about good and evil, Joyce wrote humorously on a variety of subjects: the dangers of getting shaved on Sunday ("Shave, Sir!"), risk on Wall Street ("Don't Gamble in Stocks"), people who monopolize space on street cars ("The Hog"), vulturine lawyers ("The Attorney-at-Law"). Among his books are his autobiography, *A Checkered Life*, and *Zig-Zag, Brickbats and Bouquets*, and *Truth*.

Joyce's novel appearance and warmly eccentric personality made him a nationally beloved figure. In spite of his popularity, however, after 30 years he was still preoccupied with asserting his authorship of the disputed poetry. He erected his tombstone several years before his death and had the lines chiseled into the front of it, as if the marble would carry on the argument after he was gone. Six months before he died, Joyce topped the stone with a life-size bust of himself and circulated a photograph showing him standing next to the monument, a grandfatherly hand resting on his own bronze shoulder!

Genuine Gems of John A. Joyce

Political booms burst like bloated bladders.

Personal pets with political presidential power are peevish, petulant patriots; pretenders, prevaricators, peripatetic pups for private plunder.

If you're hairy, tired and dirty,
Do your shaving on a Monday,
For the barber will be bunkoed
If he shaves you on a Sunday!
   "Shave, Sir!"

The apple butter of truth is better than the vinegar of virtue.

Sin is the Tabasco sauce of daily diet.

In the days of war, when blood flowed free,
We campaigned together, you and me;
Now who can blame me to grieve and sob
For losing my friend, my war-horse, "Bob?"
   "My War-Horse, 'Bob'"

Push and persistence puts (sic) the people on the plain of prosperity.

Wisdom, wit and work will waft you on the wings of victory.

The law, you must know, is made for the rich,
And the poor, as of old, are left in the ditch;
No matter what rights you may have to maintain,
You'll lose in the end, should you dare to "retain."
"The Attorney-at-Law"

The leader and the led will very soon be dead.

To live for one's country is more cheering than to die for it.

Vain, vain is the thought; no man ever bought
Exemption from final decay;
To live and to rot, and then be forgot—
The fate of the quick of today.
"Oak Hill"

I believe in God from will and choice, and more than all in John A.
Joyce!

Suggested Reading:

John A Joyce: *A Checkered Life*

Helen Keller

Author, Lecturer

b. June 27, 1880 Tuscumbia, Alabama
d. June 1, 1968 Westport, Connecticut
Washington Cathedral

It is a rare privilege to watch the birth, growth, and first feeble struggle of a living mind; this privilege is mine, and moreover it is given to me to rouse and guide this bright intelligence. I know that the education of this child will be the distinguishing feature of my life, if I have the brains and strength to accomplish it.

Annie Sullivan, 1887

First, a little perspective. It is 1887. Czars, emperors, kings, and queens still rule most of the world. A man named Grover heads 38 United States. Sherlock Holmes is the latest thing in mystery, the Statue of Liberty has just been dedicated, and you can send a letter to a friend for only two cents. No one talks of movies, automobiles, airplanes, or psychoanalysis; X-rays, vitamins, and penicillin are unknown. And according to law, blind and deaf persons are idiots.

On March 3, 1887, in the tiny north Alabama town of Tuscumbia, 20-year-old Anne Mansfield Sullivan meets six-year-old Helen Adams Keller. Helen is an uncontrollable blind, deaf mute. Anne, known as "Annie," herself struggling with poor eyes, has accepted a position as the child's governess, hoping at least to teach her to knit and sew. Neither is aware that they have just begun a 50-year relationship through which they will revolutionize help for, and public perception of, the deaf and blind.

Annie Sullivan was born to impoverished Irish immigrants near Springfield, Massachusetts on April 14, 1866. At about five she contracted trachoma, a disease which would plague her vision for the rest of her life. Her mother died and her father, an unskilled farm hand leaning hard on the bottle, could not care for her. Virtually orphaned, Annie bounced among rel-

Annie Sullivan

Educator

b. April 14, 1866 Agawam, Massachusetts
d. October 20, 1936 New York, New York
Washington Cathedral

atives for a time, eventually landing in the state poorhouse at Tewksbury. She was ten.

The poorhouse environment could have been something from the Dark Ages: filthy, crowded conditions; diseased, disfigured cohabitants; futility overwhelming; death ever-present. It was rumored that skins from cadavers were sold to make shoes. Annie managed as best she could at Tewksbury—it was the only home she knew—but longed to improve her life. After four years in the poorhouse, in an emotional outburst she was able to convince visiting state officials that she should receive an education. In 1880 she was enrolled in the Perkins Institution for the Blind in Boston. Ashamed of her background and total lack of formal education, Annie suffered repeated humiliations during her first year, but by 1886 she had overcome her past and was graduated as valedictorian of her class.

In the same year that Annie escaped Tewksbury and entered Perkins, Helen was born on the Keller family farm in Tuscumbia. A normal child at birth, Helen was stricken at 19 months with a mysterious fever. Days later, the fever suddenly disappeared and with it went her sight and hearing. From that moment Helen was locked within herself, unable to communicate anything other than simple needs. As she grew older she was impossible to handle, throwing violent fits brought on by the frustrations of her condition.

On the recommendation of Alexander Graham Bell, an authority on educating the deaf, Helen's parents appealed to the Perkins Institution. Having just graduated, and because she had been a brilliant student, Annie was offered the opportunity to work with the Kellers' daughter. Before taking on the child, however, Annie became proficient in the manual alphabet and spent several months studying methods previously used in teaching the blind and deaf. None had brought enough success

Annie Sullivan reading to Helen Keller. Credit: Library of Congress

to enable the subjects to function outside an institutional environment.

Although Helen later called her first meeting with Annie "the most important day I remember in all my life," the first weeks of their relationship were marked by constant battles over Helen's habit of doing anything she pleased, anytime she pleased. Firm in her conviction that "obedience is the gateway through which knowledge, yes, and love, too, enter the mind of a child," Annie forced Helen to heed her. Simple tasks such as folding a napkin triggered confrontation. Their two wills clashed; Helen's parents fled the scenes in tears. But something was changing inside Helen, and within weeks Annie's methods had become the groundwork for Helen's greatest discovery:

Someone was drawing water and my teacher placed my hand under the spout. As the cool stream gushed over one hand she spelled into the other the word water, *first slowly, then rapidly. I stood still, my whole attention fixed upon the motions of her fingers. Suddenly I felt a misty consciousness as of something forgotten—a thrill of returning thought; and somehow the mystery of language was revealed to me. I knew then that 'w-a-t-e-r' meant the wonderful cool something that was flowing over my hand. That living word awakened my soul, gave it light, hope, joy, set it free!*

and as Annie saw it:

I made Helen hold her mug under the spout while I pumped. As the cold water gushed forth, filling the mug, I spelled 'w-a-t-e-r' in Helen's free hand. The word coming so close upon the sensation of cold water rushing over her hand seemed to startle her. She dropped the mug and stood as one transfixed. A new light came into her face. She spelled 'water' several times. Then she dropped on the ground and asked for its name and pointed to the pump and the trellis, and suddenly turning around she asked for my name. I spelled 'Teacher'. . . All the way back to the house she was highly excited, and learned the name of every object she touched.

Having given Helen the key to experiencing the world around her, Annie now fed her a constant stream of information through her hand, always in complete sentences. Helen devoured it all. A childhood of empty silence suddenly exploded with anxious questions. The answers only fueled her curiosity. Annie noted, "She begins to spell the minute she wakes up in the morning and continues all day long. If I refuse to talk to her, she spells into her own hand, and apparently carries on the liveliest conversations with herself."

Think of it! Throughout history deaf and blind persons were thought to have no intellect whatsoever. Some doubted that such people had souls. Yet Helen Keller was living proof that behind the wall of her non-functioning senses was a normal, active young mind like that of any other seven-year-old. Annie's achievement was heralded as a miracle, yet it came from a simple realization: all children learn by imitation. "I shall talk into her hand as we talk into the baby's ears," wrote Annie in her diary. "I shall assume that she has the normal child's capacity of assimilation and imitation."

As news of Helen's accomplishments reached beyond Tuscumbia, she became an instant celebrity. But there was more to come. At ten she insisted on learning to speak. Unable to mimic sounds, she imitated vibrations in Annie's throat until she announced triumphantly to her parents, "I am not dumb now!" Successive steps in her development brought world acclaim. With Annie repeating class lectures in her hand, Helen attended Radcliffe, graduating *cum laude* in 1904.

Her formal education complete, Helen turned to educating others. Again breaking new ground, she drew public attention to the issue of infant blindness. Polite society had long avoided discussion of its major cause, venereal disease. Helen's efforts led to the adoption of a simple procedure (dropping a solution of silver nitrate in each eye) to eradicate what she termed "preventable blindness" in newborn babies. She wrote numerous articles and books, traveled the world speaking on behalf of the blind and deaf, counseled soldiers blinded in battle, and even appeared in vaudeville. At all times Annie was by her side.

Whenever Annie was asked about her own life story, she always pointed to Helen. "My own life is so interwoven with my Helen's life that I can't separate myself from her." As Mark Twain put it, "It took the pair of you to make a complete and perfect whole." They met each new challenge together, one the incomparable teacher, the other a determined and resourceful student. In a touching reversal of roles, Helen taught Annie to read braille when she became completely blind several years before her death in 1936.

After Annie's death, Helen continued her global crusade for the blind, meeting the most famous and influential people in each country she visited. Those whom she met were often moved by her unflagging energy and the range of her knowledge and ability. She understood and spoke several languages. She campaigned for women's suffrage and was an outspoken socialist, drawing on the ideas of Marx and Engels, whom she had read in the original German. She was the inspiration for books on courage and determination. One friend remarked, "You felt that if she had five senses she would explode, there was so much vitality."

When that vitality ran out in 1968, less than a month short of her 88th birthday, Helen was buried at Washington Cathedral, next to her beloved Teacher.

Helen was a prolific writer. Ironically, her writing skill spawned a group of unbelieving critics who felt that her impressive ability was actually that of Annie Sullivan's. Producing three full-length books after Annie's death, Helen emphatically silenced the doubters. Her writing method was not so mysterious as it may seem: she took notes in braille and wrote on a typewriter.

Helen Keller: Author

Have you ever been at sea in a dense fog, when it seemed as if a tangible white darkness shut you in, and the great ship, tense and anxious, groped her way toward the shore with plummet and sounding-line, and you waited with beating heart for something to happen? I was like that ship before my education began, only I was without compass or sounding-line, and had no way of knowing how near the harbor was.

The Story of My Life (1904)

I remember my first day at Radcliffe. . . I had looked forward to it for years. A potent force within me . . . had impelled me to try my strength by the standards of those who see and hear. I thought the professors were the embodiment of wisdom. If I have since learned differently, I am not going to tell anybody.

The Story of My Life

Every book is in a sense autobiographical. But while other self-recording creatures are permitted at least to seem to change the subject, apparently nobody cares what I think of the tariff [or] the conservation of our natural resources. . . If I offer to reform the educational system of the world, my editorial friends say "That is interesting. But will you please tell us what idea you had of goodness and beauty when you were six years old?"

The World I Live In (1908)

There are myriad sensations perceived by me of which you do not dream.

The World I Live In

When women vote men will no longer be compelled to guess at their desires—and guess wrong.

"Why Men Need Women Suffrage" (1915)

I have frequently been asked if it tires me to talk, and I have replied: "Did you ever hear of a woman who got tired talking?"

Helen Keller's Journal (1938)

Suggested Reading:

Joseph P. Lash: *Helen and Teacher.*

John F. Kennedy

35th President

>b. May 29, 1917 Brookline, Massachusetts
>d. November 22, 1963 Dallas, Texas
>Arlington

*Whizzing by at PT-boat speed came a golf cart . . . there was no
mistaking the Kennedy at the wheel. . . It was Himself.*

>Laura Bergquist,
>A Very Special President

Himself with a capital H. Did we really gush
over him like some sort of heart-throb deity? Did he do everything at "PT-boat speed?" Few Americans have generated as
much romantic idol-making as John Fitzgerald Kennedy. Like
Washington and Lincoln, Kennedy did not pass directly from
life into death; somewhere along the way he has been en-
shrined as a great American myth.

John Kennedy, "Himself," warned against the dangers of
myth: "The greatest enemy of truth is very often not the lie—
deliberate, contrived and dishonest—but the myth—persistent,
persuasive and unrealistic." The Kennedy myth certainly persists. More than two decades after Camelot was shattered—or
created—in Dallas, it intrudes on any attempt to measure the
man. Sandwiched between the respected elder, Dwight
Eisenhower, and the droopy-eyed Lyndon Johnson is the eter-
nally youthful John Kennedy, frozen forever in his prime like
an athlete photographed in his moment of glory. Columnist
James Reston seems to have grasped the point: "The heart of
the Kennedy legend is what might have been."

The first Kennedys came to Massachusetts from Ireland in
1847, seeking relief from the great potato famine. Almost from
the start politics was a family pursuit, and the generation born
to Joseph and Rose Kennedy was expected to continue it. But
John was the second of nine children—he left the political ambition to his older brother, Joe, Jr. John graduated from Har-

John F. Kennedy.
Credit: Library of Congress

vard *cum laude* in 1940, and his senior thesis was so good that he was urged to rework it for publication. Under the title *Why England Slept*, it became a national bestseller in 1940 and John entertained thoughts of a writing career.

Although he had severe back problems, Kennedy was able to get a Navy commission in World War II, commanding a patrol boat in the Pacific. On August 2, 1943, a Japanese destroyer rammed PT-109, splitting it in two. Kennedy was slammed against the cockpit wall on impact, aggravating his back. In spite of considerable pain, he managed to swim his crew to a nearby island. One crewman was too badly injured to swim, so Kennedy held a strap from the man's life preserver in his teeth and towed him for five hours to safety. After several days on the island, the survivors encountered natives. Kennedy scratched a message on a coconut, "NAURU ISL NATIVE KNOWS POSIT HE CAN PILOT 11 ALIVE NEED SMALL BOAT KENNEDY," and sent it off with the islanders, for better or worse. Three days later the haggard crew was told that help was on the way. For his actions, Kennedy was awarded the Navy and Marine Corps Medal for "extremely heroic conduct." Years later, a student asked him, "How did you become a hero?" "It was easy," he replied. "They sank my boat."

In August 1944, Kennedy learned that his brother Joe had been killed while flying a combat mission over the English channel. The role of politician now fell to him. "I told him Joe was dead and it was his responsibility to run for Congress," said Joseph, Sr. "He didn't want to, but I told him he had to." With a shock of reddish-brown hair, a brilliant smile, and the combined reputation of bestselling author and war hero, Democrat Jack Kennedy was elected to Congress in 1946. Six years later he defeated the popular Henry Cabot Lodge for a Senate seat.

The new Massachusetts senator was one of the most eligible bachelors in Washington, and thanks to the ardent match-making efforts of some friends, he met Jacqueline Bouvier, a beautiful and astute woman 12 years his junior. "I reached across the asparagus and asked her for a date," recalled Kennedy. They were married in 1953. In White House years Jackie would prove her husband's match in popular appeal. On a presidential trip to France, she was such a hit that Kennedy quipped, "I am the man who accompanied Jacqueline Kennedy to Paris."

Charisma was the word many people used to describe Jack Kennedy's ability to turn eyes, ears, and votes his way. The handsome, virile appearance, the intelligence and quick wit, the confident and candid manner—those things helped make up the Kennedy charisma. Setting him apart from other Democratic presidential candidates, they also helped bring a first-ballot nomination in 1960. But to win the presidency on his first try, Kennedy needed to project himself to a nation that did not yet know much about him. His opponent, Vice President Richard Nixon, gave him that opportunity by agreeing to a series of televised debates.

Kennedy's performance in the first televised debates in U.S. history—actually the first presidential debates in a century—is now the standard against which all others are compared. Aided by Nixon's botched make-up job and fatigued appearance in the first debate, Kennedy effectively conveyed his engaging personal style to millions of viewers. When asked about Harry Truman's use of profane language, Kennedy didn't preach about the good example a president should set, as did Nixon. His answer was light, yet it reached countless couples in their living rooms: "I really don't think there's anything that I can say to President Truman that's going to cause him to change his particular manner. Perhaps Mrs. Truman can, but I don't think I can." Turning television into a powerful political tool, John F. Kennedy had, by election day, hurdled the obstacles of Catholicism and youth and, by the slimmest margin in history, his opponent, Richard Nixon.

At the outset of his presidency, Kennedy decided to go through with a plan he had inherited for the invasion of Cuba and the overthrow of Fidel Castro's communist regime. The Bay of Pigs invasion was a disaster. Significantly, Kennedy took full responsibility for the fiasco and received an uncommon 82 percent public approval rating afterward. In 1962, Soviet missiles were removed from Cuba after he ordered a blockade of the island during the Cuban Missile Crisis. The Peace Corps and the U.S. space program were developed under Kennedy, and military advisers to Viet Nam were increased. He initiated televised press conferences, which have become obligatory for subsequent presidents. At one press conference, Kennedy was told that the Republican National Committee had adopted a resolution saying he was "pretty much of a failure." Knowing any Republican evaluation of his presidency would be negative, Kennedy broke up the hall with his response: "I'm sure it was passed unanimously."

By most accounts, Kennedy had the makings of a very good president and was destined for a second term. But on November 22, 1963, none of that mattered any more. Riding in a motorcade in Dallas, Texas, he was killed when sniper bullets struck him in the back and head. In an instant, Kennedy and the hope that had surrounded him were gone; what might have been, would never be.

In an interview with author Theodore White, the President's widow first used the phrase that would insure the myth: "At night, before we'd go to sleep, Jack liked to play some records; and the song he loved most came at the very end of this record. The lines he loved to hear were: 'Don't let it be forgot, that once there was a spot, for one brief shining moment that was known as Camelot.'" Americans loved the comparison. Once upon a time, "for one brief shining moment," we had a dashing young prince as president. No man in American history rocketed to the top quite like Kennedy. No loss has numbed this country so thoroughly. And now, no amount of reasoned analysis will make him real. And that's OK. Like Washington, like Lincoln, every now and then we need a myth like John F. Kennedy.

John Kennedy Quoted

A Plea for a raise
By Jack Kennedy

Dedicated to my father, Mr. J. P. Kennedy

Chapter I

*My recent allowance is 40¢. This I used for aeroplanes and other play-
things of my childhood but now I am a scout and I put away my
childish things. Before I would spend 20¢ of my 40¢ allowance and in
five minutes I would have empty pockets and nothing to gain and 20¢
to lose. When I am a scout I have to buy canteens, haversacks,
blankets, searchlidgs, poncho things that will last for years and I can
always use it while I cant use a cholcolote marshmellow sunday with
vanilla ice cream and so I put in my plea for a raise of thirty cents for
me to buy scout things and pay my own way more around.*

Finis
John Fitzgerald Francis
Kennedy

JFK, age 9

*Any system of government will work when everything is going well. It's
the system that functions in the pinches that survives.*

Why England Slept

*Let the word go forth from this time and place, to friend and foe alike,
that the torch has been passed to a new generation of Americans, born
in this century, tempered by war, disciplined by a hard and bitter
peace, proud of our ancient heritage, and unwilling to witness or per-
mit the slow undoing of those human rights to which this nation has
always been committed.*

Inaugural Address, 1961

*I do not believe that any of us would exchange places with any other
people or any other generation. The energy, the faith, the devotion
which we bring . . . will light our country and all who serve it, and
the glow from that fire can truly light the world.*

*And so, my fellow Americans, ask not what your country can do for
you; ask what you can do for your country.*

Inaugural Address, 1961

Khrushchev: You're an old country, we're a young country.

*Kennedy: If you'll look across the table, you'll see that we're not so
old.*

Vienna, 1961

When power leads man to arrogance, poetry reminds him of his limitations. When power narrows the area of man's concern, poetry reminds him of the richness and diversity of his existence. When power corrupts, poetry cleanses.

at the dedication of the Robert
Frost Library, Amherst College,
October 26, 1963

Suggested Reading:

Theodore C. Sorensen: *Kennedy*

William Manchester: *One Brief Shining Moment: Remembering Kennedy*

Robert F. Kennedy

Senator, Attorney General

b. November 11, 1925 Brookline, Massachusetts
d. June 6, 1968 Los Angeles, California
Arlington

Anybody here seen my old friend Bobby?
Can you tell me where he's gone?
I thought I saw him walking over the hill
With Abraham, Martin and John.

popular song, 1968

The sixties. Catch-words of the day recall an era more distant than the years: psychedelic, far-out, heavy, joint, generation gap, hang-ups. The Age of Aquarius. The quickest way to get a reading on a new acquaintance was to ask, "What do you think of the war in Viet Nam?" The movie *For Singles Only* advertised "all the fun, fury and excitement of the new boy-girl togetherness apartments," and *The Graduate* turned "plastics" into a four-letter word. White suburbanites fretted as their children spent college tuition on pass-fail sociology courses. The number of black families living in poverty was down dramatically—to 35 percent. And there was violence.

In 1968, opposition to the war was growing, black frustration was peaking, and young Americans had little faith in the unresponsive Establishment. The discontent erupted into violence with alarming regularity. Robert Francis "Bobby" Kennedy, then a senator from New York, looked at his troubled country and said, "We can do better." He had an idealistic view of what America could be and wanted to work toward making it a reality. So he entered the race for the presidency.

Bobby Kennedy did not always think of himself as presidential material. He was not as handsome, charming, or witty as his older brother John; nor could he match the future president's 1200-word-per-minute reading speed. To compensate, he

worked harder than anyone else. "Second best is a loser" was
the Kennedy family slogan, and Bobby took it to heart. Although only 5′ 9″ tall and a spare 160 pounds, he was the
starting end on the Harvard football team. "He had no right to
be on the varsity team," recalled the team captain. "We had
eight ends who were bigger, faster and had been high school
stars. But Bobby . . . worked five times as hard as anybody. . . He never let up." After breaking his leg in practice
Kennedy told no one, playing until he finally collapsed. He
later joked about his reputation for hard work: "I was the seventh of nine children. When you come from that far down you
have to struggle to survive."

Unlike John, Bobby was shy and not much of a ladies' man,
preferring to date his older sisters. He kept mostly to himself,
chewing gum and drinking lots of milk. But Ethel Skakel, a
friend of his sister Jean, had enough curiosity and all-around
zip to pull Bobby out of his shell, and in 1950 they were married. Ethel "made the difficult easy, the impossible possible,"
wrote Bobby, but he almost lost her to an impossible rival:
God. A devout woman, Ethel seriously considered becoming a
nun. In the end Bobby won out, and they produced an enormous family of 11 children.

Kennedy earned a law degree from the University of Virginia
in 1951, and in 1953, after directing brother John's successful
bid for the Senate, he became an assistant counsel on the Permanent Subcommittee on Investigations, better known as the
forum for the anti-communist fanaticism of Senator Joseph Mc-
Carthy. John had hoped that his brother would not take the
job, but perhaps to Bobby's credit, McCarthy within a year's
time wanted the FBI to investigate him.

Beginning in 1957, Kennedy conducted a series of investigations into the Teamsters Union, where the "gangster-in-labor"
was reputedly thriving. His most famous target was James R.
Hoffa, president of the Teamsters. In their first meeting, Hoffa
tried to impress Kennedy with how tough he was, issuing a
warning: "I do to others what they do to me—only worse."
Kennedy replied, "Maybe I should've worn my bullet-proof
vest." The word "ruthless" was used to describe Kennedy's pursuit of Hoffa, and it stuck long after the union boss had been
convicted. "What is it about Hoffa?" Kennedy asked an interviewer years later. "Is it ruthless to investigate the fixing of the
jury? Or misusing and embezzling millions of dollars?" Kennedy made shady union officials uncomfortable, but throughout

Robert F. Kennedy.
Credit: Library of Congress

his investigations, and later at the ballot box, the rank and file supported his efforts to eliminate union corruption.

Bobby managed John's victorious presidential campaign in 1960, expanding his reputation as an intense, tireless worker. There were cries of outrage when the president-elect named him Attorney General at the age of 35. John Kennedy joked with the critics: "I can't see that it's wrong to give him a little legal experience before he goes out to practice law." But Bobby silenced them. He brought an excellent staff to the Justice Department, made real progress in civil rights, and made the difficult J. Edgar Hoover understand that he was answerable to the Attorney General. Summing up Kennedy's tenure as the nation's number one lawyer, *The New York Times* said, "Mr. Kennedy has done much to elevate the standard."

After the disastrous Bay of Pigs invasion of Cuba, in which the entire invasion force was killed, wounded, or captured, President Kennedy included his brother in all critical policy discussions. Bobby looked on his role in the Cuban Missile Crisis as his proudest achievement. When Soviet missiles were discovered on the island, he was instrumental in the decision to blockade further shipments from Russia. A few tense days later, Nikita Khrushchev sent a letter suggesting the missiles would be removed if the United States would promise not to invade Cuba. Before a response could be made, however, a second letter was received, demanding that U.S. missiles in Turkey be withdrawn as part of any agreement. Bobby had a brainstorm: ignore the second letter while agreeing to go along with Khrushchev's initial suggestion. The gambit worked. Soviet missiles went back to Russia and nuclear confrontation was avoided.

The assassination of John Kennedy took a lot of the punch out of Bobby, but he stayed in government, winning a senate seat in 1964. In March of 1965 he decided to make the first ascent of Canada's 14,000 foot Mount Kennedy, named in honor of the slain president. Although he had never climbed a mountain, Bobby was certain he could reach the top. Only yards from the summit, the man who had faced down union bosses, J. Edgar Hoover, and Nikita Khrushchev, the man who was famous for detailed planning and research, hugged the mountain, exhausted, and asked, "What am I doing here?" Rested, he completed the ascent.

Being away from the leadership decisions of the presidency frustrated Bobby Kennedy. "We can't go on the way we're going," he told columnist Art Buchwald. The country was full of problems, violence, anger. "It is all very well to be mad at what the rest of us are not doing," he told an interviewer, "but [people] should be thinking about what they should do. Their excuse is that the government is so corrupt, that society is so corrupt, and the war in Viet Nam is so terrible, that there is nothing worth working for in the U.S. But I think there is, and we just have to go on working for it." He planned to set the example as president.

Kennedy faced an uphill battle for the Democratic nomination. He had won five of six primaries, however, when an extremist assassin killed him in Los Angeles. He was only 42. Had he lived, he surely would have remained in public life, president or not, because of his genuine concern for the fate of his country. Like the deaths of John Kennedy and Martin Luther King, Jr., 50,000 Americans in Viet Nam, lynched blacks and disappeared civil rights workers in the South, Robert Kennedy's death reminds us of a dark time in our history, and of a question Bobby once asked: "What has violence ever accomplished?"

Robert Kennedy Quoted

Each time a man stands up for an ideal, or acts to improve the lot of others, or strikes out against injustice, he sends forth a tiny ripple of hope, and crossing each other from a million different centers of energy and daring, those rivers build a current which can sweep down the mightiest walls of oppression and ignorance.

If we fail to dare, if we do not try, the next generation will harvest the fruit of our apathy—a world we did not want—a world we did not choose—but a world we could have made better, by caring more for the results of our labors.

Men and women with freed minds may often be mistaken, but they are seldom fooled. They may be influenced, but they can't be intimidated. They may be perplexed, but they will never be lost.

What it all adds up to is love. Not love as it is described with such facility in popular magazines, but the kind of love that is affection and respect, order and encouragement, and support . . . real love is something unselfish and involves sacrifice and giving.

No martyr's cause has ever been stilled by his assassin's bullet.

Suggested Reading:

Arthur M. Schlesinger, Jr.: *Robert Kennedy and His Times*
Jack Newfield: *Robert Kennedy: A Memoir*

Emanuel Leutze

Painter

b. May 24, 1816 Gmünd, Germany
d. July 18, 1868 Washington, D.C.
Glenwood

In the art world critics may praise or pan, but
the public is the final judge. Consider Emanuel Leutze's mas-
terpiece, *Washington Crossing the Delaware*. Completed in
1851, it was an instant popular hit and is probably the most
widely reproduced American painting ever. Yet almost from the
start art critics found fault with this portrait of patriotism.
Their complaints extended from a list of historical inaccuracies
to the painting's overbearing melodrama. Nevertheless, as a
touchstone of American history, Leutze's painting is, in its own
way, as important as any document in the National Archives.

Who was Emanuel Leutze? Born in Germany but raised in
Philadelphia on the banks of the Delaware, he became one of
America's great history painters. His father, a comb-maker,
died when Leutze was 14. It was while standing vigil by his father's deathbed that he decided to devote his life to art.

Like many of his contemporaries, Leutze's early training was
in figure drawing, and by age 20 he was competent enough to
support himself as an itinerant portrait painter. Looking for
more imaginative work, he soon turned to narrative painting.
The storytelling element in American art took on special importance in the mid-19th century. The opening of the West
with its seemingly unlimited potential was a tonic to painters.
As if trying physically to capture the spirit of the times, their
canvases grew with America. Leutze, in particular, specialized
in these "ten acre tapestries," focusing on dramatic events from
American history.

In 1841, Leutze went to Europe to complete his training.
The tall, red-haired American bristling with talent and energy
quickly became the star of the Düsseldorf Academy of Art. It
was in Germany that he undertook *Washington Crossing the
Delaware*, using the Rhine as his model and tracking down
every American in Düsseldorf to sit for his painting. For this

work Leutze ordered a copy of Washington's uniform to be specially made and shipped to him. Worthington Whittredge, a young landscape painter, visited Leutze and posed as the general:

Clad in Washington's full uniform, heavy chapeau and all, spy-glass in one hand and the other on my knee, I was nearly dead when the operation was over. They poured champagne down my throat and I lived through it.

Among the inaccuracies noted by critics were that Washington did not stand during the crossing, and the flag pictured was not adopted until six months later. Do the flaws detract from the artist's powerful rendering of one of the most critical moments of the Revolution? Most Americans don't think so.

Throughout the fall of 1776, Washington's army had suffered a series of defeats and was finally pushed south across the Delaware. By late December the men were demoralized and sick. Washington's plan to attack the Hessians at Trenton on Christmas day was a bold gamble that his troops still had the strength and will to mount an offensive for a seemingly hopeless cause. It was a gamble that paid off. After a two-hour battle the Hessians surrendered. Miraculously, not a single American soldier was killed. That night, Washington crossed more than a river; he crossed from defeat to victory and to the ultimate independence of the colonies. Leutze's painting celebrates this crossing, fixing it for all time in the national memory.

In 1859, the artist settled in Washington with his wife and four children and began his most ambitious work, a government commission entitled *Westward the Course of Empire Takes Its Way*, depicting the settlement of the frontier. This huge mural (20′ × 30′) pushed Leutze's artistic ability to its limit. The scene is a tangle of travelers, covered wagons, spouting geysers, and snow-clad peaks, all framed by portraits of Daniel Boone and William Clark, a view of San Francisco's Golden Gate, and, of course, the American eagle. Adding to the confusion, the painting cannot be viewed from the proper distance because it is located on a wall in the steep, southwest stairwell of the Capitol. Despite these problems, the work has an appealing raw energy which has made it popular with the public for over a century.

It was while painting the mural that Leutze made the acquaintance of President Lincoln, who followed its progress with fascination. One bitter March day the two men were walking

Washington Crossing the Delaware *by Emanuel Leutze. Washington actually sat for the ride, the flag is wrong, and James Monroe, pictured directly behind Washington, wasn't even in the boat. But few people seem to care—the spirit of history is much more popular than the facts.* Credit: Library of Congress

down Pennsylvania Avenue. Ahead of them a woman in a large hat covered with feathers slipped on the icy street and landed, unhurt, on her bottom. The President turned to the artist with a wink and said, "She reminded me of a duck—feathers on top and 'down' behind." Later, Lincoln sat for a portrait by Leutze and the two matched wits on contemporary politics.

Some of Leutze's best work is actually in portraiture. His paintings of Chief Justice Roger Taney, of Dred-Scott fame, and Nathaniel Hawthorne have won high praise. Hawthorne was delighted with the entire experience:

Leutze, when the sitting begins, gives me a first-rate cigar, and when he sees me getting tired, he brings out a bottle of splendid champagne. . . We quaffed and smoked yesterday, in a blessed state of mutual goodwill, for three hours and a half, during which the picture made really miraculous progress. Leutze is the best of fellows.

Leutze's combination of champagne and painting won him more commissions than he could take, and Hawthorne's evaluation of the artist was almost universally shared. Engaged for hours on a picture, absorbed and intent, he would suddenly break into song or set down his palette for a romp with his dog. Like his paintings, Leutze was extravagant and popular wherever he went.

On the afternoon of July 18, 1868, during an intense heatwave, Leutze collapsed in front of the Willard Hotel on Pennsylvania Avenue and died that evening. Newspapers on both sides of the Atlantic mourned his sudden death. He had shortly before been commissioned to decorate the Senate Chamber, and had made a pencil sketch of a painting, larger than anything he had previously attempted, called simply, *The Emancipation.*

In 1932, 64 years after Leutze's death, *Washington Crossing the Delaware* became the center of a national debate which reached the editorial page of *The New York Times.* The controversy surrounded preparations for the bicentennial celebration of Washington's birth. In 1930, the Metropolitan Museum of Art rolled up the painting and consigned it to the storeroom, citing as reasons its lack of artistic merit and the desire to exhibit more important paintings on its limited wall space. Immediately, there was a public outcry along with offers from numerous museums and organizations to give the painting a proper home. One letter to the *Times* suggested hanging it in Grand Central Station where, "covered by cellophane to shed the smoke and dust" it could inspire thousands of commuters daily. Another letter attacking the critics asked, "Shall we scrap our patriotic canvases and replace them with cubistic Hoovers Crossing the Potomac?" Sufficiently chastened, the Metropolitan Museum unrolled the painting once more and exhibited it at the entrance to the bicentennial exhibition which opened in February of 1932. It was a victory for the people and gave the painting new importance. The democratic ship of state, with the ghost of Washington at the helm, sailed on. Today, the painting hangs prominently in the Metropolitan—one of the best-loved artworks in America.

Suggested Reading:

Ann Hawkes Hutton: *Portrait of Patriotism*

UNCROWNED
CHAMPION
©

A 1935 publicity photo of Joe Louis. The caption's boast was no longer necessary after he won the heavyweight title in 1937. Credit: Library of Congress

Joe Louis

Boxing Champion

b. May 13, 1914 Lafayette, Alabama
d. April 12, 1981 Las Vegas, Nevada
Arlington

Muhammad Ali: "Joe, you really think you coulda whupped me?"
Joe Louis: "When I had the title, I went on what they called a bum-of-
the-month tour."
Ali: "You mean I'm a bum?"
Louis: "You woulda been on the tour."

OK kid. Now you got your shot at Joe Louis and the World
Heavyweight Championship. You've earned it, too. The press is calling
the Brown Bomber's latest series of title fights the "Bum-of-the-Month"
campaign, but you're no bum. Anyway, Louis is so slow you'll run
circles around him. Yeah. Better watch those hands, though.
Locomotive power at jet speed. Nervous? Sure. You can't help but
admire sombody who whipped Hitler's golden boy Schmeling in two
minutes. That guy was dumb! He went around calling Joe names, got
him mad. Wasn't that a night! Schmeling walked into a one-man
bombing raid! Never had a chance. People all over the country were
celebratin', bangin' pots and pans in the street like it was New Year's
Eve. Joe's not invincible, though. He's been knocked down, out of the
ring, even. It's just that guys don't put the finishing shiner to him. But
you won't let him get away, will ya?

The seventh child born to a cotton sharecropper
and his wife, Joe Louis Barrow spent his early childhood in a
windowless shack near Lafayette, Alabama. When Joe was
three, his father deserted and the family moved north to De-
troit, following the promise of jobs in the burgeoning auto industry. As a teenager Joe was urged by his mother to develop a
manual skill, and for a while he studied cabinetmaking. But
one of the few professions that offered blacks a steady income
during the Depression was music, so she gave him a dollar a
week for violin lessons. Unknown to her, Joe skipped his music
lessons—his massive hands hardly fit the violin—and used the

money to pay for sparring lessons at a local gym. When his mother found out where her weekly dollar was going, instead of getting upset, she encouraged Joe to pursue this unexpected "manual" skill.

In 1932, Joe Louis fought his first amateur bout. He had dropped the name Barrow, perhaps because he never knew his father, and took the name Louis into the ring as his own. Louis's boxing debut is memorable only in light of his later successes—he was dropped to the canvas six times in two rounds by an ex-Olympian. There was some reward in the beating, though. In amateur boxing everyone received checks redeemable for merchandise, losers as well as winners. Considering the options—the Ford plant, cabinetmaking, the violin—the seven dollars Louis received was incentive enough to continue boxing. He went on to take the winner's check ($25) in 54 amateur fights, 43 by knockout.

On Independence Day, 1934, Joe Louis turned pro, sending a fighter named Jack Kracken to the canvas in the first round. At 6' 1½" and a shade under two hundred pounds, Louis was not the biggest of heavyweights, but he was among the strongest. Deliberate rather than mercurial on his feet, he could be hit, sometimes going down for a mandatory eight-count. Once, he was knocked out of the ring. But he invariably rose to end the fights with a few well-placed haymakers—his talent was in those huge hands. In his first two years as a professional, Louis did not lose in 26 bouts. The fights averaged four rounds apiece, with 22 of them knockouts. Called the "Brown Bomber" for his race and slugging power, Louis won the world heavyweight title by knocking out Jim Braddock on June 22, 1937.

Not since flamboyant Jack Johnson had finally been overcome by a "White Hope" in 1915 had a black man donned the heavyweight crown. Johnson had taken great pleasure in antagonizing whites, flaunting his white female companions and belittling his opponents. After his defeat, the white-controlled boxing world excluded blacks from title opportunities. Then came Joe Louis. He was Johnson's opposite: soft-spoken, friendly, mannered. He called his trainer "sir." Louis carefully avoided any comparisons with Johnson, yet at the same time, he gave the black man a sense of pride, clearly dominating the most prestigious sporting class of his time while refusing to be stereotyped as a grinning watermelon-eater.

On June 22, 1938, Louis fought a rematch with Max

Schmeling of Germany, a former champion and the only man to have beaten him as a pro. Schmeling was Hitler's pet specimen of the "master race." From his camp came slurs and insinuations that Louis was a dumb animal. Meanwhile, Nazi Germany was poised for war, giving the fight a backdrop of adversary nations in symbolic confrontation. President Roosevelt is supposed to have urged Louis to victory by squeezing his biceps and saying, "Joe, we need muscles like yours to beat Germany." Added to the pre-fight boil was the sentiment from some American whites that any white champion, even a Nazi, was better than a "colored" one. "Max Schmeling said a good German could beat any colored man in the world," recalled Louis. "That night I felt like every colored man in the world."

More than 70,000 people were on hand at Yankee Stadium to witness what has been called "the most dramatic two minutes in the history of the ring." Millions more attended by way of radio. Only moments before entering the ring, Louis told a friend, "I feel wonderful. I'm afraid I might kill him." Grinning to the crowd at ringside, Schmeling was woefully unprepared for what was about to befall him. As the bell sounded Louis wasted no time, cutting into Schmeling viciously, by one count landing more than 40 punches. The challenger managed only two of his own. He went down four times before the referee mercifully ended the fight at 2:04 of the first round. With a frightening power and unarguable finality, Joe Louis had pulverized the theory of a master race. For black America, it was a time for jubilation, a night to walk tall down main street.

Beginning in late 1940 Louis took on a series of aspirants to the heavyweight title in his legendary "Bum-of-the-Month" campaign. For nearly a year he fought a title bout every month, knocking out each opponent. In all, he made 25 title defenses, more than the combined total of the eight champions who had preceded him.

In 1942, Louis donated the purses from two title fights, totaling over $80,000, to the Army and Navy Relief Funds. When the United States entered World War II he volunteered but declined a commission, preferring to be a "plain, ordinary GI." As with many celebrity recruits, the Bomber contributed to the morale of the troops, staging nearly one hundred boxing exhibitions for two million soldiers world-wide. After spending four of his prime earning years in the Army, Louis defended his title four more times, retiring as the undefeated champion in 1949.

Shortly after his retirement, Louis ran into the undisputed governmental heavyweight—the IRS. Louis had managed his career earnings poorly and now the tax collectors added up the debt for him: $1.25 million. Characteristically, he did not attempt to avoid his responsibility. He returned to boxing in an effort to pay his tax bill, winning eight bouts and losing two, the last to the young champion-to-be, Rocky Marciano. The IRS intercepted most of his income, including $667 he inherited when his mother died. For 15 years Louis struggled to satisfy Uncle Sam. He tried professional wrestling, but a 320-pound behemoth jumped on his chest, breaking ribs and bruising muscles in his heart. He tried a night club routine and drew this review: "As a song and dance man, he was a tremendous boxer." Finally, in 1965, the IRS announced to Congress, "We have gotten all we could possibly get from Mr. Louis, leaving him with some hope that he can live. His earning days are over."

Throughout his ordeal with the tax man, public sentiment was heavily in Louis's favor, based mostly on the purses he donated to relief and the substantial income he gave up in order to serve his country in World War II. Safely squared with the IRS, Louis settled into a job as a "greeter" in a Las Vegas casino. The work suited his genial nature well.

In a profession rife with unsavory types, Joe Louis carried himself with true dignity. His life had been a hard one: shoeless and hungry as a child, four marriages, financial and mental health problems. But he did not draw on any of this to encourage sympathy. The sports writer Red Smith noted, "Not once . . . was Louis known to utter a word of complaint or bitterness or offer an excuse for anything. To be sure, he had nothing to make excuses about." Unlike other champions, Louis did not endlessly trumpet his prowess in the ring. He spoke few words, but they were often well chosen. When one fighter boasted how he would speedily avoid the Bomber's punches, Louis made this concise analysis before knocking him out: "He can run, but he can't hide." Louis was too good a boxer to be kept from the world championship, and his character made him the right kind of man to win it. Joe Louis was an American hero who deserved the laurels.

Hey kid, you all right? Wake up, the fight's over. What do you mean, "What happened?" You were so fast you forgot to look where you were goin'. Ran right into a howitzer. You should've seen it! Fantastic! Oh, sorry. Look, don't feel so bad. Years from now you can tell your grand-

children about this. Dress the story up a little. You know, like you had him worried for most of the first half of the first round. Then you got careless. Let him off the ropes, so to speak. But you did it. Yes, sir. You fought Joe Louis, the greatest heavyweight of all time.

Feeling better?

Suggested Reading:

Gerald Aston: *". . . And a Credit to His Race;" The Hard Life and Times of Joe Louis Barrow, a.k.a. Joe Louis*
Barney Nagler: *Brown Bomber: the Pilgrimage of Joe Louis*

George C. Marshall, considered by many the greatest American soldier and statesman of the 20th century. Credit: National Archives

George C. Marshall

Soldier, Statesman

b. December 31, 1880 Uniontown, Pennsylvania
d. October 16, 1959 Washington, D.C.
Arlington

Succeeding generations must not be allowed to forget his achievements and his example.

Winston Churchill

George Catlett Marshall was a rare man. Had he wanted glory, it was his for the taking. Had he wanted to be president, he probably would have been. But he wanted only to serve his country well as a soldier and a statesman, and to leave glory-seeking and partisan politics to others. There is no denying that Marshall served his country brilliantly: As a soldier, he directed the victorious Allied effort of World War II; as a statesman, he set in motion the program known as the Marshall Plan, which revitalized a devastated post-war Europe. As a result, George Marshall became the only military man ever to win the Nobel Peace Prize.

After high school in Uniontown, Pennsylvania, Marshall attended Virginia Military Institute, where the memory of Confederate General Stonewall Jackson oozes out of every brick and stone on campus. Because of his northern accent, Marshall endured more than his share of hazing during his first weeks as a cadet. As part of his unofficial "initiation" into the corps, he was forced to squat naked over the blade of a bayonet anchored in the floor. He was weak from a bout with typhoid and after a few minutes collapsed onto the blade, which stuck in his groin. Coming within an eyelash of a very serious injury, the young cadet bore the pain so well in the following weeks that the rest of the corps took him in like any other good ol' southern boy. The ability to conceal pain and emotion later during some of the most anxious times in modern history won Marshall the confidence of all who knew him.

Marshall graduated from VMI in 1901 and was granted an Army commission the following year. (Unlike West Point cadets, VMI graduates were not automatically accepted into the Army. They had to be tested and recommended.) He got married just before leaving for his first assignment in the Philippines, and then listened in dismay as his bride revealed on their wedding night that a weak heart prevented her from having any children. Marshall drew praise for his ingenuity during World War I, especially for moving a half million men and 2700 artillery from one front to another in organizing the Meuse-Argonne offensive. General John Pershing, impressed with the talented officer, made him his personal aide from 1919 until Pershing's retirement in 1924. In 1927, Marshall became assistant commandant of the Infantry Training School at Fort Benning, Georgia. If an officer or instructor at the school displayed admirable qualities, Marshall entered the man's name in a notebook in case he might need to call on reliable help at some point in the future.

In 1939, President Roosevelt made Marshall Army Chief of Staff, promoting him from brigadier to full general. Marshall held that post throughout World War II, during which time he oversaw the growth of the Army from 200,000 to 8.3 million men. Referring to his notebook of outstanding officers, he placed effective leaders in important commands. He also formed a superb staff. Every morning at 9:00 A.M. aides poured into his office carrying maps and charts. Using information received only hours before, they presented the war situation in every part of the world. More than a few observers of these daily performances were dumbstruck at the enormity of what they saw, and of the awesome responsibilities of General Marshall.

When the decision had been made to cross the English Channel and invade France, the presumed commander of the operation, called "Overlord," was George Marshall. He was the best man for the job. Churchill believed it. Stalin believed it. Roosevelt did, too. But who would replace Marshall as director of those daily global reviews? Who could comprehend and coordinate the world war effort, if not George Marshall? Two men were capable enough to run Overlord—Marshall and Eisenhower. But only Marshall could run it all. However, Roosevelt was keenly aware that whoever commanded the invasion would become as famous as Ulysses S. Grant and Robert E. Lee, while the Chief of Staff might remain historically anonymous. He felt the decision should be left to Marshall. With the selfless dignity that made him so revered by his contemporaries, Marshall refused to make the choice for Roosevelt. "I was," he later said, "utterly sincere in the desire to avoid what had happened so much in other wars—the consideration of the feelings of the individual rather than the good of the country." For the good of the country, America's best soldier stayed in Washington while Eisenhower became a national hero.

Many powerful people in Washington saw a future president in George Marshall. But when approached, Marshall made it emphatically clear that he was not interested in party politics. However, there is ample evidence that his influence in the White House was substantial. Roosevelt was relieved that Marshall did not go to London to command the European invasion, telling him, "I didn't feel I could sleep at ease if you were out of Washington." Harry Truman, who called Marshall "the greatest of the great," placed such blind trust in his judgment that many of the "bucks" that presumably stopped at Truman's desk were handled entirely by Marshall.

Marshall resigned as Chief of Staff in November 1945. Sixty-five years old, he was looking forward to a little rest after spending four tense years directing the Allied victory. But Truman wouldn't let him have it. A week after resigning, Marshall's profound sense of duty made him agree to help the President try to solve growing problems in China. Ultimately, however, even he could not bring the Communists and the Nationalists together, and in December 1946, he gave up the mission and came home. A month later, Marshall again answered Truman's call and agreed to become Secretary of State. In his two years in this position, Marshall helped create the National Security Council, the North Atlantic Treaty Organization (NATO), and the Organization of American States (OAS). His greatest accomplishment, which earned him the Nobel Peace Prize in 1953, was the European Recovery Act, better known as the Marshall Plan. Under this plan, billions of dollars were poured into 16 war-ravaged European nations to help some two hundred million people get back on their feet. The idea was inspired in no small way by Marshall's belief that the Soviet Union was looking forward to the economic and political collapse of Western Europe.

In poor health, Marshall quit as Secretary of State in 1949, but Truman kept him nearby by arranging his appointment as president of the American Red Cross. In 1950, with a war heating up in Korea, Truman called on him once more, this time to be Secretary of Defense.

Finally, in 1951, Marshall retired for good. He turned down a million dollar offer to write his memoirs because he felt he must tell the truth, and by so doing would necessarily embarrass a great many famous people. And when he died, George Marshall was buried simply, with "no fuss," as he had instructed. His grave is very unspectacular, especially for an American whom one biographer has called "probably the greatest man since Lincoln." Tour buses glide by the gravesite many times each day. Sometimes the guides mention his name, too often they don't. Even with a cemetery map his stone isn't easy to find. It takes a little time and effort to find Marshall's grave, just as it takes a little time and effort to appreciate his achievements. Unlike Grant and Lee, Roosevelt and Eisenhower, George C. Marshall is one of American history's great secrets. Once you know it, you feel like telling everybody.

Suggested Reading:

Forrest C. Pogue: *George C. Marshall*
Leonard Mosley: *Marshall: Hero for Our Times*

Audie Murphy

World War II Hero

> b. June 20, 1924 Kingston, Texas
> d. May 28, 1971 Roanoke, Virginia
> Arlington

January 26, 1945, Holtzwihr, France—Snow covers the frozen ground. Baby-faced second lieutenant Audie Murphy spots six German tanks churning toward his company's position followed by waves of infantry. The attack is furious. Murphy orders his men to retreat, remaining alone to direct artillery by field radio. The effort seems lost, but as he turns to run he sees a burning tank destroyer with a ready machine gun atop it. Radio in hand, Murphy ignores the flames, mounts the destroyer and spends the next hour guiding artillery fire and picking off 50 German soldiers advancing on three sides. Not until the enemy has retreated and he has attempted to rejoin his men does Murphy notice the pain of a wounded leg. Nonetheless, he organizes a counterattack which eventually drives the Germans from Holtzwihr.

This scene would be recounted a thousand times in newspapers and magazines, in living rooms and on front porches. The gallantry of 20-year-old Audie Murphy captured the imagination of a grateful America ready to carry him home on its shoulders, cheering the deeds of a classic war hero.

Before the war, home for Murphy had all the elements of folk legend. One of 11 children, he grew up in what he described as "an honest-to-God shack." His sharecropper father deserted the family and his mother died a few years later. At 17, struggling to support his orphaned brothers and sisters, Audie learned to make every bullet count when hunting and could kill a rabbit on the run with a slingshot.

In June 1942, Murphy lied about his age to join the Army and went on to become the most decorated combat soldier of World War II, receiving the Medal of Honor for the action at Holtzwihr. In all, he received 24 U.S. medals, three French, and one Belgian. He was wounded three times.

When Murphy's picture appeared on the cover of *Life* magazine after the war, it caught the eye of movie star James Cagney who invited him to Hollywood. Arriving in uniform (technically, he would not be out of the Army until the next day), Murphy was met at the airport by Cagney and a swarm of reporters and autograph hounds. Audie blushed at requests for his signature and winced whenever someone called him a hero. Although his fame and all-American good looks gave him tremendous star potential, Audie had two strikes against him: a Texas twang thick enough to whittle with a knife, and no formal drama experience. Murphy himself summed up his screen ability in two words—"no talent." In spite of the drawbacks, with Cagney's support he took acting classes and eventually starred in almost 40 films, including John Huston's *The Red Badge of Courage* (considered his best film) and *To Hell and Back*, the autobiography of his war experiences. Playing himself in the World War II production, Murphy often confused reality and fantasy during the filming, reliving events of a decade earlier only to find that it was all for the camera, no one was dying this time.

Though Audie achieved considerable fame in Hollywood, he disliked the pretentious social swirl and hated squeezing into a tuxedo. California may have been his residence, but Texas was always his home. Audie never forgot his roots and visited his friends and family in the Lone Star State whenever he could.

Besides acting, Audie wrote a number of country and western songs. His "Shutters and Boards" has become a C & W classic and has been recorded by Jimmy Dean, Porter Waggoner, and Dean Martin.

Audie Murphy was killed in a plane crash in the mountains near Roanoke, Virginia, while on a business trip. He was buried in Arlington near the Tomb of the Unknown Soldier, but the standard military marker above his grave is too small to list all his decorations of honor. Murphy himself gave most of his medals to children. Although he was honored by three countries for his courage and daring and was credited with killing 240 German soldiers, Audie Murphy didn't think anyone who ever fought a war really survived it. He had nightmares for many years, and could get to sleep only after putting a loaded pistol under his pillow.

Suggested Reading:

Harold B. Simpson: *Audie Murphy, American Soldier*

Simon Newcomb

Astronomer

b. March 12, 1835 Wallace, Nova Scotia, Canada
d. July 11, 1909 Washington, D.C.
Arlington

*Simon Newcomb's life-work is of monumental importance to
astronomy.*

Albert Einstein

Most people think computers are something
new. Actually, we've been using them for well over a hundred
years. Of course, they were much slower then, but they were
accurate and dependable. They were also reasonably inexpen-
sive and required little programming and no electricity.

They were young mathematicians.

Simon Newcomb was a math wizard whose first formal contact with astronomy came in 1857, when he was hired as a
"computer" for the Nautical Almanac, the annual tables of celestial movements used by navigators and astronomers. Forty
years later he had been recognized throughout the world not
only as the greatest American astronomer of his time, but as
his nation's foremost scientist as well.

Signs of Newcomb's mastery over numbers came early in his
childhood in Nova Scotia. At four, he became so engrossed in
"puzzling out" addition and multiplication problems that his
parents worried he would calculate himself "out of his head."
He revealed a superb sense of reasoning, constantly trapping
his father with planned series of questions, like a clever lawyer
examining a witness:

"Father, does form mean shape?"
"Yes."
"Does everything have form?"
"Yes."
"Then how could the world be without form when God first made it?"

Young Simon was also absentminded and "pitiful" when it

Simon Newcomb, who called celestial mechanics "the world of sweetness and light." Credit: Library of Congress

came to physical coordination. All of this convinced his bewildered parents that he was insane, and they seriously considered sending him to an asylum because of this supposed "derangement" and "imbecility." Fortunately, Simon showed evidence of being a normal child in his teens, satisfying his parents that he had overcome his "disease."

In 1851, Newcomb was apprenticed to a highly reputed herb doctor. However, the boy soon learned that the "doctor" was no more than a quack, whose theory of life was "this world is a humbug, and the biggest humbug is the best man." After two wasted years as a virtual servant—he never saw a patient treated—Newcomb escaped, making a rugged journey by land and sea to Salem, Massachusetts, where he was met by his father. A short time later they moved to Maryland, near the Naval Observatory in Washington, D.C. It was there that he found his calling.

Fascinated by the complexities of the universe, Newcomb taught himself astronomy. He loved the challenge of calculating where a star or planet had been one hundred thousand years ago and where the shadow of an eclipse would cross the earth at any time in the future. In 1861, as civil war enveloped the country, Newcomb was commissioned and assigned to the Naval Observatory, where he concentrated on questions of planetary orbits and motions of the moon.

In 1877, Newcomb was appointed Director of the Nautical Almanac, and soon thereafter launched the 20-year project that produced a body of work hailed as "priceless treasures of astronomical literature." The project was a recalculation of the motions of the planets of our solar system. By 1877, telescopic observations of planetary movements were more accurate than ever before, making tables based on earlier sightings obsolete. Recalculating the tables for the sun, moon, and nine planets required tens of thousands of new, precise observations from all over the world, as well as the patience and determination to complete all the necessary computations. Since every planet attracts every other planet (gravity), plotting the daily course of all the heavenly bodies involved equations of mind-boggling complexity, often running on for many pages. After 20 years, Newcomb and his team had completed the observational work and much of the mathematical interpretation, but so massive was the amount of data collected that a full interpretation of it was never completed (Newcomb would have appreciated the speed of modern computers!). The resulting tables were used throughout the world for over 50 years.

Newcomb's project loomed as the most difficult ever undertaken by an astronomer. By successfully grappling with such an overwhelming task, he transferred world leadership in mathematical astronomy from its longtime home in Paris to Washington, adding greatly to the intellectual prestige of the United

States at the same time. France acknowledged Newcomb's achievements in 1896 by electing him an officer in the Legion of Honour.

Newcomb made many other contributions to science. In 1878, he set up mirrors on opposite banks of the Potomac and performed experiments leading to a calculation of the speed of light that is very close to that of later findings. It disturbed Newcomb that younger astronomers were shifting away from his mathematical approach to the stars near the end of the 19th century. When a longtime friend, Samuel P. Langley, left astronomy to pursue the dream of manned flight, Newcomb became so irritated that he made his now-famous pronouncement: "Man will never fly."

Curiously, Simon Newcomb was an astronomer who disliked the "night work" of making telescopic observations. But on at least one occasion, a telescope came in handy for observing an historic event. The following quote comes from a letter to this wife, dated December 6, 1884:

Well! the Washington monument was finished this afternoon! They had the finishing touch given with some little ceremony which I watched from my window with a telescope. It consisted in Col. Casey setting the aluminum point of the pyramid with his own hand. When it was in place he leaned over the platform, at a greater height from the ground than a human being ever before stood on a fixed point, and waved his hand. A flag was at once raised, and cannon began to peal forth.

Suggested Reading:

Simon Newcomb: *Reminiscences of an Astronomer*

John Howard Payne

Actor, Playwright

b. June 9, 1791 New York, New York
d. April 9, 1852 Tunis, Tunisia
Oak Hill

Pioneers sang it as they crossed the prairies in covered wagons. Seafarers sang it for courage as they rounded Cape Horn. Farmers sang it by bright hearths in the dead of winter. For millions of people throughout the world, "Home, Sweet Home" was one of the most beautiful and moving songs of family and brotherhood ever written. Today, we hear it most often in sentimental dramas and westerns, yet this simple melody of the pleasures of home still has a unique power to draw people together. It is one of the ironies of history that the author of "Home, Sweet Home," John Howard Payne, was an expatriate vagabond who died alone on the shores of the Mediterranean, far from those he loved.

Howard Payne was more than a songwriter. For much of his life he was one of America's leading actors and dramatists, writing over 60 pieces for the stage. Indeed, his famous song was actually penned for a play which he sold outright, largely to repay debts. Payne never received a penny in royalties for all the millions of copies of "Home, Sweet Home" printed, bought, and sung.

A child prodigy, Payne was just 15 when his play *Julia, the Wanderer* was staged in New York. The title set the tone for his own life. The youthful author spent the next seven years traveling up and down the East Coast as an actor and writer. In Boston he became the first American to play Hamlet and appeared opposite Elizabeth Poe (Edgar Allan's mother) in *Romeo and Juliet*. Greeted enthusiastically wherever he went, Payne was by all accounts America's first stage idol.

In 1813, Payne set sail for London, hoping to make his fortune as a playwright. Critical success, however, came more quickly than financial security. Although England's top theaters vied for his work, debts piled up faster than he could repay them. To dodge persistent creditors, Payne disappeared for several months, surfacing in Paris in spring 1822. That Christmas Eve he wrote his sisters in New York from an attic in the Palais Royal:

My yearnings toward Home become stronger as the term of my exile lengthens. I long to see all your faces and to hear all your voices. 'Twould do me good to be scolded by Lucy and to see Anna look pretty and simple and sentimental. . . I feel the want of you, in this strange world, for though I am naturalized to vagabondage, still it is but vagabondage. . . I long for a home about me.

Early the following year, *Clari, the Maid of Milan*, with "Home, Sweet Home" in the score, premiered in London and John Howard Payne was suddenly internationally famous. The compelling pathos of the opening night is a matter of record. Even the theater manager's wife "wept torrents" at the production. The press was unanimous in its praise and Payne returned to London a hero.

Following the triumph of *Clari*, Payne collaborated with his good friend Washington Irving on several successful comedies, and courted Mary Shelley, the "wild wife" of the poet who had recently drowned in Italy. The love affair between the author of "Home, Sweet Home" and the author of *Frankenstein*—never a likely match—was finally broken off by Mrs. Shelley, who was obsessed by the memory of her husband. Payne's rival was the ghost of a poet he had never met. Undoubtedly stung, the handsome playwright remained a bachelor for the rest of his life.

Payne was greeted by a plague of cholera on his return to the United States in 1832. The New York papers hailed his homecoming, but the city was shuttered and quiet and it was several months before a proper reception—a benefit performance of excerpts from his plays—could be held. The gala evening was capped by a novel toast to "the pleasure of receiving—Payne!"

The 20 years in Europe had taken their toll and the author felt like a stranger in the land of his birth. While touring the country to raise subscriptions for a theatrical journal he planned, Payne was arrested in Tennessee and nearly shot as an Indian sympathizer. True, he had taken the Indians' side concerning the removal of the Cherokee beyond the Mississippi, and had written several articles appealing for justice, but he was far from the agitator local officials suspected. In Kentucky, Payne spent a memorable evening with George

In this contemporary broadside, John Howard Payne is pictured above his "Home, Sweet Home." Credit: Library of Congress

Keats, brother of the poet John Keats. "He indulged me with a glance at their private correspondence," Payne wrote, "including much of the unprinted poetry of that distinguished brother." Payne came away with four unpublished poems and material for an article about his surprise discovery, but money for the magazine—the reason for his western trip—never materialized. America was still too young and too busy growing to care much about the arts.

In August 1842, with the help of Daniel Webster, Payne was appointed U.S. Consul to Tunisia. Not exactly the position he would have chosen, it did relieve his constant financial worries and gave him a chance to visit London enroute to his new post. The old haunts of his theater days struck him like a strange dream. In one empty street he found a blind beggar playing "Home, Sweet Home" on a flute. For the next ten years, off and on, North Africa was Payne's home. Nearly forgotten by his countrymen, he died in 1852 and was buried in a cemetery overlooking the harbor and the ruins of Carthage.

The wanderings of John Howard Payne would have ended there had it not been for William Wilson Corcoran, a Washington philanthropist, who conceived a plan to bring the famous songwriter back to his native land. In 1883, 31 years after his death, Payne's body was transferred from Tunis to Washington, D.C. When the casket arrived, President Chester A. Arthur led a delegation of dignitaries to Oak Hill Cemetery, and John Philip Sousa and his Marine Band provided music. As the casket was lowered into the ground, the melancholy verses of "Home, Sweet Home" echoed over the tree-shaded hillside.

One final, yet oddly appropriate, confusion occurred before Payne could rest. Corcoran had commissioned a marble bust of the songwriter to be placed on the grave, but when the statue was unveiled revealing Payne with a full beard, no one could remember if he had ever worn one. Embarrassed officials quickly hired a stonecarver who neatly chipped off the offending whiskers. Later, the Mathew Brady photograph of Payne used as a model by the sculptor was examined and clearly showed that, indeed, the famous playwright <u>was</u> bearded. To this day the bust remains clean-shaven. Although everyone at Payne's final ceremony knew the famous song by heart, no one really knew the man who wrote it.

Home, Sweet Home

'Mid pleasures and palaces, though we may roam,
Be it ever so humble, there's no place like home!
A charm from the sky seems to hallow us there,
Which, seek through the world, is ne'er met with elsewhere

(Chorus)

Home, ho-ome, sweet, sweet home—
There's no place like home, there's no-o place like home!

An exile from home, splendor dazzles in vain,
Oh, give me my lowly thatched cottage again;
The birds singing gaily that came at my call,
Give me them with the peace of mind, dearer than all

(Chorus)

(Below are two additional verses printed on the program for the "Reinterment of the Remains of John Howard Payne")

How sweet 'tis to sit 'neath a fond father's smile
And the cares of a mother to soothe and beguile;
Let others delight 'mid new pleasures to roam,
But give me, Oh! give me, the pleasures of home

To thee I'll return, overburdened with care;
The heart's dearest solace will smile on me there;
No more from the cottage again will I roam,
Be it ever so humble, there's no place like home.

Suggested Reading:

Grace Overmyer: *America's First Hamlet*

Robert Peary in his arctic furs. Credit: Library of Congress

Robert Peary

Arctic Explorer

b. May 6, 1856 Cresson, Pennsylvania
d. February 20, 1920 Washington, D.C.
Arlington

*T*igi-su—"The Big Nail"—that's what the
Eskimos called it. Why anyone would want to travel to the
middle of a sea of drifting ice to find this imaginary point was
a mystery to them. Surely, one had to be touched with mad-
ness. And perhaps Robert Peary was. His only desire, around
which he built his life, was to be the first man to reach that
point, the North Pole; to be the first to stand on top of the
world. He finally claimed victory over the Big Nail on April 6,
1909, but he touched off a controversy that still rages today.

Peary's family was from Portland, Maine, and he grew up exploring the many nooks of neighboring Casco Bay. His father
died when he was three, leaving his mother to watch after the
mischievous youth. After graduating from Bowdoin College, the
tall, wiry engineer got a job with the Navy. But steady work
made his restlessness more acute. "I don't want to live and die
without accomplishing anything," he wrote home. His first taste
of the Arctic came in 1886 when he and a friend attempted to
be the first to cross Greenland. Although unsuccessful, the trip
fired Peary's ambition. "I <u>must</u> have fame," he told his mother,
"I cannot reconcile myself to years of commonplace drudgery."
Her reply had the ring of prophecy: "If fame is dearer to you
than anything else, what am I to say? I think if you should
look at the matter calmly and dispassionately you would be less
enthusiastic—such fame is dearly bought."

In a Washington, D.C., hat shop, Lieutenant Peary met Matthew Henson, the black ex-seaman who became his assistant
for 22 years. Henson loved the thrill of adventure almost as
much as Peary and was the only American with Peary when he
made his dash for the Pole.

Between 1891 and 1906, Peary led numerous expeditions to
the Arctic, each more daring than the one before. Peary's re-
sourcefulness earned him high praise from veteran Arctic trav-

elers. He kept his parties small and specialized in traveling light, Eskimo style. Building igloos as he went rather than carrying heavy tents and wearing a suit of thick fur which doubled as a sleeping bag, Peary could move relatively quickly over long distances.

But the cold took its toll. During a reckless winter journey with Henson in 1899, Peary got frostbite. As Henson ripped off the explorer's rabbit-skin boots, several toes from each foot snapped off at the first joint and clung to the hide. "Why didn't you tell me your feet were frozen?" Henson cried. "A few toes aren't much to give to achieve the Pole," Peary replied stoically. The Pole, however, remained elusive, and back in the United States Peary's family was growing lonely. His daughter complained, "I have been looking at your pictures, it seems, ten years, and I am sick of looking at them. I want to see my father. I don't want people to think me an orphan." His wife, realizing she had married a man married to the Arctic, was emotional: "Oh Bert, Bert. I want you so much. Life is slipping away so fast—pretty soon all will be over." Peary, too, felt life slipping away, but he was concerned for a different reason.

On the afternoon of July 6, 1908, Peary set sail from New York. This time the trip had one simple objective: reach the Pole. He was 52 years old and knew that for him it was The Big Nail or bust. His plan seemed foolproof: five sledge parties would travel ahead, breaking trail and dropping supplies for Peary's sledges. The lead parties would systematically fall back until, about 130 miles from the Pole, Peary's group would be alone for the last spurt.

In Greenland, the news was distressing. The Eskimos told Peary that Frederick Cook, another American explorer, had left seven months earlier for the Pole. True, no one had heard from him since, but Cook was as glory-hungry as Peary, and few doubted that he wouldn't return.

At dawn on February 28, with the temperature hovering at $-50°F$, the expedition began snaking its way across the frozen sea. The blowing snow stung their faces like shattered glass. Chopping through pressure ridges and crossing open water on dangerous ice rafts, the men made steady progress.

When all of the lead groups had turned back, Peary, Henson, and four Eskimos began the final assault. The last lap, Peary wrote, was "a glorious sprint with a savage finish . . . the dogs galloping along and reeling off the miles in a way that delighted my heart." (Henson's memoirs paint a radically different picture, describing a maze of floebergs and drift ice, and a party so exhausted they were dropping in their tracks.)

On April 6, Peary took his first solar reading in five days and surprised everyone by announcing that they had arrived. But Henson sensed that something was amiss. When he attempted to check the final reading, Peary wouldn't let him. When he tried to congratulate his boss, Peary turned away.

After the obligatory flag-raising and photographs, they pointed their sledges south, toward home. Peary was physically spent; weak and shuffling, his face a mask of pain, he rode much of the way.

Back in civilization, Peary learned that Frederick Cook had returned, claiming to have reached the Pole almost a year earlier. Cook was being honored as the Arctic hero, but in a statement to the press, Peary calmly attacked: "Cook has simply handed the public a gold brick." When the evidence was examined, most scientific organizations agreed. The record of Cook's field observations was conspicuously missing and the two Eskimos who had traveled with him said they were never out of sight of land.

In 1911, after Congress had scrutinized his records, it was determined that Peary had reached the Pole. But the controversy would not die. During the congressional investigation, cracks appeared in Peary's story. Why hadn't he taken readings for the last five days before reaching the Pole? How could he be sure of his direction without readings? How could he have traveled so far, so fast? Why hadn't Henson been allowed to verify his readings at the Pole? To some, these cracks became chasms and made Peary's tale as unstable as the polar ice cap itself.

Since Peary's death in 1920, a number of scientific studies have been made of the race to the Pole. Most conclude that neither Peary nor Cook came within one hundred miles of striking The Big Nail. But if the verdict is in, the case is not closed. In the popular mind, Robert Peary is still credited as the first man to reach the North Pole. Who knows? Perhaps he was.

Suggested Reading:

Frank Rasky: *The North Pole or Bust*
John Edward Weems: *Peary: The Explorer and the Man*

John J. Pershing

General of the Armies

b. September 13, 1860 Laclede, Missouri
d. July 15, 1948 Washington, D.C.
Arlington

In 1881, an advertisement appeared in a small town newspaper in northeastern Missouri:

On July 15th there will be a competitive examination for the appointment of a cadet at the United States Military Academy at West Point. All honest, strong, God-fearing boys of this district may take part.

Just a few inches of type, but it started John Joseph Pershing on one of the most impressive military careers in American history; a career that took him from the Indian Wars to the World Wars and finally earned him the rank of General of the Armies, an honor he shared only with George Washington.

There was no silver spoon at Pershing's birth. His father was a railroad foreman and almost as soon as he could walk, John started working himself. His earliest memories were of a mob of Confederate bushwhackers shooting up the Unionist homes in his town, and later, of the ragged, silent soldiers wandering home after Appomattox.

After teaching for two years in Prairie Mound, Missouri, Pershing entered West Point just under the maximum age limit of 22. Though diligent in his studies, he was neither the best disciplined nor the most scholarly of the cadets and graduated in the middle of his class in 1886.

One of his first assignments was to South Dakota where, as part of the Sixth Cavalry, he helped cordon off Sitting Bull and the Ghost Dancers. The Sioux unrest culminated in the infamous massacre at Wounded Knee. Pershing took no part in the atrocities on the snow-covered reservation, but a brief skirmish with Kicking Bear and his band several days later provided his first combat citation.

In 1899, Pershing sailed to Manila, where, off and on for the next 14 years, he struggled to subdue the rebellious Moro tribe. "Black Jack" Pershing, as he came to be called for his black jack-tough discipline, eventually earned the respect of the Moro chiefs, and his stunning military successes won him promotion from captain to brigadier general, passing him over 862 senior officers.

On his return to the United States, Pershing was put in charge of an expedition into Mexico to hunt down Pancho Villa. Soon after arriving at his Texas headquarters, he got word of a terrible tragedy. Pershing's wife and family, who were staying temporarily at the Presidio in San Francisco, had been the victims of an early morning fire; only his six-year-old son survived. Pershing received the news without emotion. After a long silence, his granite-like jaw jutted out, "Is that all? Is that everything?" he inquired of the orderly who had read him the telegram. From then on, Pershing's work became his life, and reserve and self-control—some said coldness—became a mark of his character. Any grief or loneliness he felt was hidden behind the wall of his West Point training.

The Villa episode—more of a Mexican goose chase—was a test of Pershing's patience and ability to follow orders. Mexico had been in the throes of revolution since 1910 and in the chaos, Pancho Villa, a semi-literate cattle rustler, had gained control of northern Mexico with his hard-riding band of irregulars. His Robin Hood style of robbing the rich and distributing the loot to the poor had made him a hero among the local peasants.

On March 9, 1916, Villa's army raided Columbus, New Mexico, killing a number of Americans. Six days later, Black Jack Pershing rode into Mexico giving chase. But the outlaws had vanished. For almost a year Pershing and Villa played hide and seek. With little else to do, Pershing policed the countryside, drilled his troops, and waited for orders to return home. Finally, in February 1917, the last American soldier crossed the Rio Grande back into the United States. Although Villa had been neither captured nor punished, in retrospect, the expedition served one grim purpose: it gave Pershing and the American forces a rigorous field test just two months before the United States entered World War I.

Within hours after Pershing's arrival in Washington on May 10, 1917, President Woodrow Wilson put him in charge of the American Expeditionary Forces being sent to Europe. Initially,

General of the Armies John J. Pershing takes time out to pose with a raw recruit—Babe Ruth. Credit: Library of Congress

only a limited involvement was planned, but when Pershing realized that France was near military collapse, he began laying the foundations for an American army that would total nearly three million men. Pershing's job was to build that army, transport it across the Atlantic Ocean, and defeat the Germans, the most powerful, smooth-running fighting machine the world had known. The General's upright bearing, devotion to duty, and tireless energy set the standard. "Every private a Pershing" became the Army's motto. With the chorus of "Over There" still echoing in their ears, the doughboys poured into France.

Although American troops began by reinforcing the French and British armies, Pershing argued forcefully for preserving the integrity of the U.S. Army as a separate fighting unit. After the Americans proved themselves at the second battle of the Marne, General Pershing was given his independent command.

The most important engagement fought by the Americans as a separate fighting force was the Meuse-Argonne offensive. The objective, in Pershing's words, was "to draw the best German divisions to our front and consume them." After 47 days of bitter, often hand-to-hand fighting, the Americans burst through the Hindenburg line. Ten days later, on November 11, 1918, the war was over.

When the General arrived back in the United States, the "Pershing Boom" was on. In recognition of his achievement in assembling almost from scratch a superb national army, Congress recreated Washington's rank of General of the Armies and awarded it to Pershing. There was even talk of nominating him for President.

After serving as Chief of Staff for three years and helping to draw up the blueprints for today's modern army, Pershing retired in 1924. Fifteen years later, when Germany was again terrorizing Europe, Pershing's call to train four hundred thousand new troops was dismissed as the rantings of a senile warmonger. The American public had a short memory.

Black Jack's last years were spent as the unwilling captive of doctors and nurses at Walter Reed Army Hospital. His health had deteriorated so that he needed frequent medical attention, but his mind was as sharp as ever and the boring hospital routine finally roused him to action. One day, when the doctors looked in, they found his bed empty. One of them remembered Pershing's fondness for the stately old Carlton Hotel where he had often stayed, and a search party was sent to investigate. Sure enough, the General had checked into his favorite suite and was found sitting before the remains of a feast of roast duck. "You've found me, have you?" snapped the veteran. "Well, you can remove yourself from my sight now while I finish my brandy." The doctor withdrew, and after a few minutes a proud Pershing appeared, ready to return to the hospital. The expedition had been short but memorable; Pershing had again emerged victorious. Historians would duly record that it was the only time General Pershing went A.W.O.L.

Suggested Reading:

Frank E. Vandiver: *Black Jack: The Life and Times of John J. Pershing*
Richard O'Connor: *Black Jack Pershing*

Albert Pike

Poet, Masonic Leader

b. December 29, 1809 Boston, Massachusetts
d. April 2, 1891 Washington, D.C.
House of the Temple

It was said of Pike that he was a giant in body, in brain, in heart and in soul.

Henry Miller

Albert Pike packed enough talents and accomplishments into his 81 years for a dozen average men. Poet, adventurer, lawyer, soldier, mystic, and Freemason, Pike's genius was many sided, reflecting the spirit of his times. Yet today, outside the circle of Freemasonry, few people recognize his name.

The life of Albert Pike nearly spanned the 19th century. Born the same year as Abraham Lincoln, Pike was raised in the heart of New England. He was described as "six feet tall with proportions of a Hercules and the grace of Apollo, a face and head massive and leonine, recalling some sculptor's dream of a Grecian God." Although he passed the entrance examination at Harvard, Pike was unable to come up with the tuition and so set out to educate himself. Thirty-five years later, after achieving fame as a poet and lawyer, Pike proudly accepted the honorary masters degree Harvard offered him.

In 1831, Pike went west, following the footsteps of Zebulon Pike, a distant relative who had discovered Pike's Peak 25 years earlier. The West of the 1830s was largely unmapped and inhabited only by Indians, trappers, and traders. Traveling mostly on foot and living off the land, Pike was awed by what he saw and fascinated by the people he met. One trapper showed him the trick of leaving a buffalo leg on an ant hill overnight. The ants would strip the flesh and the next morning the bones could be roasted and cracked to get at the marrow.

Finally, after a hair-raising, five hundred mile trek through

Albert Pike, a "sculptor's dream of a Grecian god." Credit: Supreme Council of Freemasonry

Comanche country, Pike turned up at Fort Smith, Arkansas. Ragged, shaggy, and penniless, he took a teaching position with a salary in pigs and began writing the poetry which brought him international acclaim. When his group of poems, "Hymns to the Gods," appeared in 1839, Edgar Allan Poe declared, "there are few of our native writers to whom we consider him inferior." Poe's own work is thought to have been influenced by Pike.

In 1835, with little formal training, Pike was admitted to the bar and soon had a thriving legal practice. Frontier law was almost a form of rural entertainment. Using skill and showmanship, Pike could hold a courtroom spellbound with tall tales carefully woven into his arguments. His wide range of experiences, coupled with his polished oratory and sheer bulk, made him one of the most sought after lawyers in the state.

In 1859, Pike had the unique pleasure of attending his own wake. When a man named Albert Pickett died, word circulated that Albert Pike had passed away. Immediately, plans were made for an elaborate wake in Pike's honor. When Pike showed up alive some of his friends decided the festivities should proceed. With Pike waiting in the adjoining room, flowery eulogies were read and toasts were made to his memory. When the guests were well primed, Pike appeared Lazarus-like and regaled them with his adventures in hell.

When the Civil War broke out, Pike cast his lot with the South and became the center of a famous war-time controversy. Given the rank of brigadier general by Jefferson Davis, he was appointed to oversee the Indian territories. Pike was opposed to using Indians outside their own land, but in 1862 he was called on to supply a Cherokee brigade for regular duty. At the battle of Pea Ridge (March 7–8), the Indians under Pike's command gained notoriety by scalping some of the Union dead. Pike formally apologized but refused to take responsibility for the atrocities, claiming the Indians were ordered into action against his will. Northern newspapers sensationalized the story, inflating the number of scalps taken and dubbing Pike a half-breed general. The flurry of publicity in both the North and the South caused him to resign in bitterness.

After the fall of Little Rock to Union forces, Pike loaded a wagon with books and disappeared into the Ozark Mountains to think and write. *Morals and Dogma*, the product of Pike's solitary retreat, appeared eight years later. It has been said that this unusual book is either the work of a genius or a madman. Begun as a revision of the ceremonies and rituals of the Ancient and Accepted Scottish Rite of Freemasonry, an organization Pike had joined in 1850, it ended up as much more. Mixing flights of poetry with musings on love, religion, history, politics, and economics, it is a big, mysterious book that probably few people have read and fewer can claim to understand.

In 1869, Pike moved to Washington, D.C., where he devoted most of his energy to the study of Freemasonry. This ancient fraternal society teaching brotherhood, justice, and freedom of religion and expression arrived in America in the early 1700s. Though it is not a secret society, it does have secrets, such as passwords and handclasps. Many of our founding fathers, including George Washington, Benjamin Franklin, and Paul Revere, were bound by the mystic tie of Freemasonry. Pike was fascinated by its obscure origins dating back to the Middle Ages, when highly skilled stone masons built the beautiful cathedrals that dot the European countryside. Pike's contribution to the development of Freemasonry in the United States is unparalleled; to date he is recognized as this country's greatest Masonic scholar and philosopher.

While in Washington Pike fell hopelessly in love with the alluring young sculptor, Vinnie Ream. Vinnie had captured the hearts of many influential men in the Capital, and Pike, though nearly 40 years her senior, was no exception. "You are of those for whom men go mad or pine away in despair and die," he wrote her. In 1872, Vinnie modeled a bust of Pike with shoulder-length hair and flowing beard. Her interest, however, was more friendly than loving, and following her marriage to Richard Hoxie, Vinnie saw little of Pike.

Pike's will directed that when he died he be cremated and the ashes sprinkled around the roots of two acacia trees which grew in front of the Temple of the Supreme Council of Freemasonry in Washington. The Council, however, decided on a burial at Oak Hill Cemetery. In 1944, Pike's body was transferred to the crypt in the new Temple, an imposing structure modeled after the Mausoleum at Halicarnassus, one of the seven wonders of the world. But Pike, always restless in life, is also restless in death. Some people have seen his ghost wandering the stairways of the Temple at night.

Suggested Reading:

Robert Duncan: *Reluctant General*

John Wesley Powell

Grand Canyon Explorer

> b. March 24, 1834 Mount Morris, New York
> d. September 23, 1902 Haven, Maine
> Arlington

August 13, 1869:
We are now ready to start our way down the Great Unknown. We have
but a month's rations remaining. We have an unknown distance yet to
run, an unknown river to explore. With some eagerness and some
anxiety and some misgiving we enter the canyon below. . .

So begins John Wesley Powell's account of the
first boat trip down the longest, wildest whitewater route in the
world: the Grand Canyon. No white man had ever explored the
length of the Colorado River. Fabulous stories were told of falls
that dwarfed Niagara, spots where the river vanished into the
ground, and cliffs that towered ten thousand feet on either
side. It was the last empty spot on the map and Powell was determined to fill it in.

The son of a Methodist minister who emigrated from England
to carry the gospel to the frontier, Powell grew up traveling
west. His homemade education was good enough to allow him
to teach science in Illinois, but when the Civil War broke out
he promptly enlisted to fight against slavery. Powell lost his
right arm at the bloody battle of Shiloh when his battery made
a crucial stand. What for many would be a serious handicap
failed to dull Powell's restless energy. Back in Illinois he re-
sumed teaching and scientific study, and began planning his
Colorado River odyssey.

On May 24, 1869, while the inaugural run of the first transcontinental railway was still steaming across America's heartland, Powell and a rough-and-ready band of nine volunteers
shoved off into the swift current of the Green River in Wyo-
ming and was quickly lost from view. Although the purpose of
the voyage was to advance science, adventure was what they
found. Rowing and dragging four specially built boats down

John Wesley Powell talking with a Paiute Indian in northern Arizona, c. 1869. Credit: U.S. Geological Survey

more than a thousand miles of foaming rapids and winding canyons, the expedition met drama and hardship at every turn:

June 8, Canyon of Lodore:
One of the boats capsizes and is dashed to pieces. With it go a third of the rations and the crew's clothing.

June 16, Hell's Half Mile:
The campfire, spread by a whirlwind to some dead willows, forces the party to abandon camp in confusion, losing most of the bedding and utensils.

June 18, Echo Park:
While climbing out of the canyon to take observations, Powell nearly falls to his death. Clinging to the sheer rock wall with his one hand, unable to go up or down, he lunges desperately at some long under-wear lowered from above and is saved.

August 28, Grand Canyon:
Mutiny! Three men refuse to continue on what they believe is a doomed voyage. Leaving the canyon, they are never heard from again—presumed killed by Indians.

Finally, on August 30, bone-weary and half starved, the expedition emerged at the junction of the Colorado and Virgin rivers in southern Nevada where three men and a boy were peacefully fishing. The remaining rations consisted of 10 pounds of moldy flour, 15 pounds of dried, fermenting apples, and 70 pounds of coffee. But the ordeal was over; the Canyon was conquered!

Word of Powell's success spread quickly. Newspapers throughout the country carried sensational stories of the one-armed veteran's heroic journey. Realizing that the scientific results of the expedition were inadequate, Powell took advantage of the publicity to organize a second voyage. Congress supplied ten thousand dollars, and in the spring of 1871 Major Powell again set out from Green River City. This time the trip was unexpectedly cut short by high and dangerous water. Even Powell was heard to cry out, "By God, boys, we're gone!" as the boats plunged down the cataracts. It was the only time Powell refused a challenge, but it probably saved his life.

In 1872, Powell settled in Washington, D.C., and used his knowledge of the West and his personal influence to organize the National Geological Survey, the Bureau of Ethnology, and the National Geographic Society. During the 1870s and 1880s he became an important spokesman for the careful development of the West. He proposed laws to organize irrigation districts and pasturage districts. More important, he persuaded government officials that the West could not be settled along patterns used in the East. The West needed an environmental and scientific approach to settlement and farming. Powell's proposals were creative answers to the regional problems of the vast expanse beyond the Mississippi.

In 1894, after 13 years as Director of the Geological Survey, Powell retired. The nerves in the stump of his right arm had regenerated, causing him great pain and making it difficult for him to work. When he died in Haven, Maine, shortly after the arrival of the 20th century, an era died with him. He was one of the last generation of explorers who had gazed on the unmapped reaches of the United States and after seeing them, put his energy and knowledge to work for the good of the country and the new lands he had seen.

Suggested Reading:

Wallace Stegner: *Beyond the Hundredth Meridian: John Wesley Powell and the Second Opening of the West*

John Wesley Powell: *The Exploration of the Colorado River and Its Canyons*

Pushmataha, the Indian General. Painting is by Charles Bird King.
Credit: Smithsonian Institution

Pushmataha

Choctaw Indian Chief

> b. 1764? Mississippi
> d. December 24, 1824 Washington, D.C.
> Congressional

"**I** had no father, I had no mother. The lightning rent the living oak, and Pushmataha sprang forth." At least that's what the Chief of the Choctaw Indians told inquisitive white men. Not only could he speak eloquently of his origin, but his gifted tongue also helped Pushmataha maintain a peaceful relationship between white settlers and his tribe; no small feat. Respected as a courageous warrior and clever negotiator, Pushmataha allied his people with the new Americans against the British in the War of 1812, and then outwitted his friend Andrew Jackson in 1820 at the Treaty of Doak's Stand.

Born in what is now Mississippi, Pushmataha earned his warrior's reputation while still in his teens. During a day-long battle with the Osage, young Pushmataha disappeared, returning to camp after dark. Jeered by the other braves as a coward, Pushmataha produced five Osage scalps and invited anyone who could improve on his heroics to continue laughing. The other warriors listened in silence as he recounted his single-handed attack on the enemy's rear.

Pushmataha's reputation grew over the next two decades as he led periodic raids through Arkansas, Oklahoma, and Texas. He became chief of all Choctaws in 1805. Unlike other tribal leaders, Pushmataha cultivated friendly relations with encroaching settlers and in 1811 thwarted Tecumseh's effort to organize an Indian Confederacy to push the whites back to the East. Pushmataha reasoned that battling the greater numbers and weapons of the whites could only lead to the extinction of his people.

Convinced that Choctaw survival depended on the survival of a friendly American nation, Pushmataha and five hundred of his warriors aided General Jackson in the War of 1812. Pushmataha distinguished himself in the Pensacola Campaign, leading his warriors with strict discipline. Thereafter he was known among whites as the "Indian General."

Jackson and Pushmataha became good friends, but in 1820 they were pitted against each other during negotiations for an exchange of Choctaw and U.S. lands, later known as the Treaty of Doak's Stand. Pushmataha was aware that Jackson had very little knowledge of the U.S. territory (now parts of Arkansas and Oklahoma), so he described it as a wasteland, insisting that the Choctaws would need a vast area to insure good hunting. Jackson got the eastern Choctaw lands he sought, but gave up much more good territory than he realized. When the treaty was complete Pushmataha acknowledged the agreement with the phrase "Sia Hoka," meaning "it is agreed." Widespread use of "Hoka" by settlers may have been the origin of the term "O.K."

Not content with the treaty Jackson signed, the Monroe administration wanted to renegotiate. Pushmataha reluctantly came to Washington in the fall of 1824 to discuss what he had believed would be the last treaty with the whites. Many weeks passed without a settlement. Cold weather and a diet of rich foods deteriorated Pushmataha's health. He became seriously ill on December 23 and died within 24 hours.

Andrew Jackson led a procession of two thousand people to Congressional Cemetery where Pushmataha was buried with full military honors. A cannon salute fulfilled his burial request, "let the big guns be fired over me."

During the Doak's Stand negotiations Pushmataha called the U.S. territory he would acquire a wasteland. Later, when the Americans wanted some of it back, he described the land as a paradise. He explained the contradiction like a shrewd businessman: "I was buying then and I am selling now, which as you know, makes a difference."

Suggested Reading:

Anna Lewis: *Chief Pushmataha, American Patriot*

Vinnie Ream

Sculptor

b. September 25, 1847 Madison, Wisconsin
d. November 20, 1914 Washington, D.C.
Arlington

*I seemed to be in a singular and indescribable vessel moving toward a
dark shore. The peculiar thing about it is that I've had this same
dream before, and each time it preceded great events—Antietam,
Murfreesboro, Gettysburg, and Vicksburg. . .*

President Lincoln was speaking to General
Grant, almost unaware of the young woman with brown, flowing
curls who stood nearby putting the finishing touches on a clay
bust of the nation's leader. It was the afternoon of April 14,
1865, and in a few hours the meaning of Lincoln's strange
dream of the night before would be tragically clear.

Vinnie Ream was one of the last people to visit the President
before his assassination at Ford's Theatre. For five months the
President had allowed her to come daily during his lunch to
model a statue of him. It was a great honor for her, an experience that changed the life of one of the first women sculptors
in the United States.

Born in Madison, Wisconsin, Vinnie moved with her family
to Washington during the Civil War. To help her parents make
ends meet, she got a job at age 14 at the Post Office where she
sorted mail sent to and from the front.

In 1863, a new vista was opened to Vinnie when a con-
gressman, impressed by her interest in sculpture, invited her
to visit the studio of the noted sculptor Clark Mills. "As soon
as I saw the sculptor handle the clay, I felt at once that I too
could model and, taking the clay, in a few hours I produced a
medallion of an Indian chief's head." Mills was impressed and
offered her free lessons with the warning that sculpture was a
demanding career—particularly for a young woman with Vinnie's slight build—and that she would probably have to work
years before producing anything truly satisfying. But Mills's re-

alism couldn't dampen Vinnie's enthusiasm. While Mills was casting the bronze figure of Armed Freedom to be placed on the Capitol Dome, Vinnie watched, questioned, and listened.

Although she saw the sadness of war throughout Washington, from the wounded soldiers filling the makeshift hospitals to the gaunt look on Lincoln's face, Vinnie's dream of becoming a great sculptor, of creating beauty, did not die. Soon, she was busy making busts of such famous figures as Thaddeus Stevens, an outspoken opponent of slavery, George Armstrong Custer, later killed at the Little Big Horn, and Horace Greeley, the newspaper editor and abolitionist.

Late in 1864, Vinnie arranged to begin work on the bust of the President. Initially, he had refused, claiming he was too busy to sit for an artist. When he found out the sculptor was a 17-year-old girl who, like himself, had been raised in a poor family on the frontier, Lincoln sympathized with Vinnie and agreed to the project.

Though she saw him for only half an hour a day, Vinnie got to know and admire the President in all his moods. "I was modeling the man in clay," she said later, "but he was being engraved still more deeply in my heart." The night he was assassinated she stood until dawn near the house across from Ford's Theatre where Lincoln struggled for his life. Her bust of Lincoln, virtually finished at the time of his death, pleased her admirers so much that in 1866, when Congress authorized the creation of a life-sized marble statue of Lincoln to be placed in the Capitol rotunda, Vinnie Ream was awarded the ten thousand dollar contract, the first time a federal commission had ever gone to a woman.

Essentially self-taught and with little experience, Vinnie was suddenly asked to produce a full figure of a national hero. She was used to working with moist clay that yielded to the touch, but had never worked with marble. Instead of the artist's spatula, she would have to learn to wield a mallet and chisel.

The award was not without controversy. One irritated newspaper attacked her ability and morals, describing Vinnie as:

a young girl of about twenty who has been studying her art for a few months, never made a statue, has some plaster busts on exhibition, including her own, minus clothing to the waist, has a pretty face, long dark curls and plenty of them. . . She sees members at their lodgings or in the reception room at the Capitol, urges her claims fluently and confidently, sits in the galleries in a conspicuous position and in her

Seventeen-year-old Vinnie Ream and her bust of Abraham Lincoln.
Credit: Library of Congress

*most bewitching dress, while those claims are being discussed on the
floor, and nods and smiles as a member rises. . .*

But Vinnie brushed off the accusations by replying cooly,
"These people know nothing of art."

Vinnie was given a studio in the basement of the Capitol and
there completed a plaster model of Lincoln. Then, accompanied by her parents and her two pet doves, and with the
model stowed safely in the ship's hold, she set sail for Italy to
sculpt the marble version.

Choosing the purest white marble from the quarries at Car-
rara, and working in Rome under the guidance of an Italian
stonecutter, Ream completed the Lincoln statue in 1870 and
returned to the United States. In January of the following year
the statue was unveiled at an impressive ceremony in the ro-

tunda. Senator Trumbull, who had helped secure the contract for Ream, spoke:

It was fitting that he who, by his own unaided effort, rose from obscurity to the highest position in this land, and who went down to his grave mourned by the civilized world, should have his features transmitted to posterity by one who, like him, had nothing but her head and her hands to urge her forward.

The statue and the sculptor were greeted with thundering applause. Senator Carpenter of Wisconsin commented, "Of this statue as a mere work of art, I am no judge . . . but I am able to say, in the presence of this vast and brilliant assembly (most of whom knew the slain President well) that it is Abraham Lincoln all over." It can still be seen just inside the west entrance to the rotunda.

Vinnie was now at the height of her powers. In 1872, she completed an impressive bust of her close friend Albert Pike, the eccentric poet and Masonic scholar. Then, three years later, she won a government contract to do a statue of Admiral Farragut, the Civil War hero, to be erected in Farragut Square. Cast from the propeller of the Admiral's flagship, the bronze statue was unveiled in 1881 with President Garfield accepting the piece for the nation. While working on the Farragut statue, Vinnie met and married Richard Hoxie, a friend of the Admiral's who was in the Army Engineers.

Requests for Mrs. Hoxie's work were now coming in from all over the country. In 1906, the state of Iowa commissioned a statue of its Civil War governor, Samuel Kirkwood, for Statuary Hall in the national Capitol. Because of poor health, Vinnie was able to complete the work only with the aid of a rope hoist and boatswain's chair rigged by her husband.

Vinnie was well aware of her role in opening up the profession of sculptor to women. Addressing the International Convention of Women five years before her death, Vinnie asked:

Why shouldn't a woman be a sculptor? Her brain is as great, her thoughts as tender, her fingers as skillful as those of men. She does not hesitate to climb the scaffolding, to mount the ladder—and often from it she ascends to fame.

Suggested Reading:

Freeman H. Hubbard: *Vinnie Ream and Mr. Lincoln*
Gordon Langley Hall: *Vinnie Ream*

Walter Reed

Surgeon

b. September 13, 1851 Gloucester County, Virginia
d. November 23, 1902 Washington, D.C.
Arlington

To those who are gone already and here's to the next to go!

Toast offered at meals by members of Reed's yellow
fever medical team

New Orleans is known for its festive atmo-
sphere, but during the summer of 1853 it was more like an
open morgue. Yellow fever infected nearly half the inhabitants,
killing 11,000. Caskets were stacked in the cemeteries and the
stench of death hovered throughout the city. The ebb and flow
of the disease was measured by the number of burials recorded
daily. In 1878, another epidemic raged up the Mississippi and
Ohio river valleys, leaving 20,000 people dead. With a high
fever, unbearable headaches, and the horrible "black vomit," a
result of severe internal bleeding, yellow fever was the terror of
the Americas until Walter Reed, using human volunteers for
his experiments, succeeded in isolating its ally and sole con-
veyor, the mosquito. Reed's triumph over yellow fever was the
climax of a personal quest for medical knowledge that also ac-
cented the strides made in medical science in the late 19th
century.

So little was known when Reed entered medicine that he was
able to earn a medical degree at 17 from the University of Virginia after only nine months' study. Eager to learn more, he
completed a second degree a year later at Bellevue Hospital in
New York. Medical internships did not exist in 1869, but by
starting his career in several New York hospitals, young Dr.
Reed saw the full range of human injury and illness. At one
point he worked in a children's hospital where one in every
three patients died. He managed to withstand the strain of that
job, but the quackery that flourished under Tammany Hall and

Boss Tweed was almost unbearable to him. Medical ignorance was rampant among the vainglorious men who masqueraded as doctors in their fine clothes and elegant carriages; so many of them prospered, apparently without any ethical misgivings, that Reed nearly quit medicine in disgust.

Seeking broader experience and a change from the big city, Reed joined the Army Medical Corps in 1875. His first assignment was a frontier outpost in the Arizona desert, about as far as anyone could get from the bustle of New York. Before leaving, he married Emilie Lawrence, a girl he had known since his teens; and she bravely agreed to accompany him into Apache country. The couple's harrowing 23-day wagon journey through the scorched Southwestern landscape was a true test of their love.

Over the next 15 years, Reed moved almost annually to posts all over the country, acquiring a good knowledge of Indian life in the process. As a diversion, he wrote a magazine article extolling certain features of the Apache lifestyle. He especially appreciated, from a modest distance, the custom of Apache women who allowed their freshly washed clothes to dry on their bodies. Once, he treated a small Indian girl who had been severely burned and abandoned. The girl, called Suzie, joined the family after her recovery and helped care for the younger Reed children for the next ten years.

In 1890, although the concept of medicine as science was new and not highly regarded, Reed persuaded the Army to allow him to study at the Johns Hopkins Medical School in Baltimore. In 1893, he was made a professor at the new Army Medical School in Washington and was also appointed curator of the Army Medical Museum, which gave him access to the mass of research information stored there.

An outbreak of malaria among soldiers at Washington Barracks and Fort Myer, Virginia, in 1896 offered Reed an early opportunity to investigate the spread of infectious disease. It turned out that only enlisted men had been infected, even though they ate, drank, and lived much the same as officers. But Reed discovered that the soldiers frequently slipped off to the city along a path through stagnant swamps and marshes. After he halted this activity, the malaria subsided, and Reed presumed that bad air in the marshes must have been responsible for the outbreak.

At the end of the 19th century America's eye had turned to the Caribbean and beyond, most notably to the narrow isthmus of Panama. France had abandoned a seven-year effort to build a canal connecting the Atlantic and Pacific oceans there after yellow fever had decimated the work force. It had become clear that any attempt by the United States to build a canal would require control of yellow fever. In 1900, when "Yellow Jack" broke out among American troops in Cuba, the time was right for a thorough investigation aimed at checking the disease. Charged with that task, Major Walter Reed was sent to Havana.

For 20 years Dr. Carlos Finlay of Havana had argued to anyone who would listen that mosquitoes were the means by which yellow fever was spread. But he had never proved his claims, and most people passed him off as a well-intentioned kook. They preferred theories about polluted air or contaminated garments and bedclothing. Reed, who had not previously considered Finlay's assertions worth pursuing, now decided to look more closely.

Experimenting with mosquitoes was not easy; the only animals known to be susceptible to yellow fever were humans. Reed concluded that the only effective way of testing the mosquito theory was to use human volunteers. He drafted a consent form that began "The undersigned understands perfectly well that in the case of the development of yellow fever in him, that he endangers his life. . ." The public outcry was immediate, and Reed was pronounced a "medical amateur" engaged in "savagery." Fortunately, all of the 22 volunteers who contracted yellow fever survived. But Dr. Jesse W. Lazear, a valuable member of Reed's medical team and a close friend, was accidentally bitten, contracted the disease, and died.

Lazear's death provided clues to the mosquito theory, but cool fall weather was bringing the yellow fever season to an end. Reed had to act fast. He worked late into the night when others were exhausted. When a fierce storm destroyed many of his caged "birds," Reed dragged his fellow investigators down to a garbage dump hunting for more larvae. He was delighted to find the tiny pouches in standing water in old, discarded toilets.

By following carefully designed experiments, Reed was able to isolate the female *Aëdes aegypti* mosquito as yellow fever's accomplice. He also tested the theory that contaminated clothing could transmit the disease. Three courageous volunteers spent three weeks sleeping in night shirts and bedclothes that were drenched and encrusted with the black vomit, urine, and sweat of fever victims. Aside from the chills they got each time they crawled between the contaminated sheets, none developed symptoms of yellow fever.

As a result of Reed's research, Havana underwent an intense fumigation and drainage program intended to wipe out the mosquito population. Within a year the city was free of the terrible disease that had been a part of Cuban life for most of two centuries. Several years later, a successful extermination campaign paved the way for construction of the Panama Canal.

In spite of Reed's findings, there were many doctors and scientists who were reluctant to accept the mosquito research as conclusive, still clinging to theories they had supported for decades. However, some conversions came very quickly. In one instance, a group of doubting physicians toured a laboratory where mosquitoes were kept for continuing studies. When some of the insects accidentally got loose in the room, the doctors panicked, fighting each other to get out the door. It seems there were no skeptics in a room full of mosquitoes!

Having weathered torrents of public criticism, Reed the "amateur" had been vindicated. Sadly, he did not have long to enjoy his fame or further advance the science of medicine. Weak from overworking, Walter Reed died of appendicitis and peritonitis on November 23, 1902. The huge Army medical center in Washington, D.C., that bears his name stands as a memorial to his work. The same could be said of the Panama Canal.

Suggested Reading:

William B. Bean, M.D.: *Walter Reed: A Biography*

Mary Roberts Rinehart

Mystery Writer

b. August 12, 1876 Allegheny, Pennsylvania
d. October 12, 1958 New York, New York
Arlington

She was mistress of the Macabre; murder was her business. For 50 years her chilling tales of corpses and criminals dominated the bestseller lists. She was America's answer to Agatha Christie and Dorothy Sayers. She was Mary Roberts Rinehart, and she was an extraordinary woman.

Born in the year of Custer's Last Stand, Mary Roberts was raised in a struggling middle class family in Pittsburgh. Her childhood provided unforgettable story material: the mute boy next door talking on his hands to his mother; the butcher who ran amuck, killing his wife with a meat axe; the shadowy roomers slipping up and down the stairs of her house; her frustrated father-inventor's suicide in a hotel in Buffalo. Throughout these hard early years, Mary watched, learned, and remembered.

Four days after graduating from nursing school she married Stanley Rinehart, a young doctor, and was soon pregnant with the first of three sons. Mrs. Rinehart found housework, caring for the children, and helping her husband with his medical practice took much of her time but gave her little personal satisfaction. In frustration, Rinehart turned to writing as an outlet. The manuscript of her first published piece, written while she was recovering from diptheria, was carefully fumigated before being sent off. Fortunately, it didn't spread the disease; but interest in her work quickly grew.

In 1903, a stock market panic erased the family's small savings and the resulting financial crisis gave Rinehart the excuse she needed to break the traditional taboo against working wives. Writing every day at a rickety card table, she completed 45 poems and stories within a year and earned almost $1,800.

The first and most popular of her novels, *The Circular Staircase*, appeared in 1908 and had all the hallmarks that made Rinehart famous. Mixing murder and suspense with humor and romance, Rinehart created a new kind of mystery writing. Her subjects, she claimed, were ordinary people entangled in terrifying situations.

In *The Circular Staircase*, five lives are snuffed out while Miss Rachel Innes, a witty, middle-aged spinster, solves the mystery of a secret room in an old summer house she has rented. The tale ends with a pair of weddings and Miss Innes itching for new excitement. "To be perfectly frank, I never really lived until that summer," she declares. "I shall advertize to-morrow for a house in the country, and I don't care if it has a Circular Staircase."

Critics praised Rinehart's technique as the first advance in crime fiction since Arthur Conan Doyle invented Sherlock Holmes. And the public loved it. By 1910 her family was well out of the red, and Rinehart had become a one-woman factory turning out stories almost faster than they could be published. Responding to her complaint that she couldn't find a pen quick enough to keep up with her thoughts, the Parker Pen Company came to the rescue with a custom-made fountain pen.

When World War I broke out, the *Saturday Evening Post* asked Rinehart to go as America's first female war correspondent. She had already established herself as an independent woman unwilling to fit the Victorian mold, and now her desire for adventure pushed her on. After a "grave conference" with her husband, the 38-year-old author sailed to England.

Although official policy kept journalists from the front, Rinehart used her nursing background to reach Belgium, and late one night she visited no-man's land, two hundred yards from the German lines. "I have done what no woman has done before," she wrote, "and I am alive." Later she interviewed King Albert of Belgium, Queen Elizabeth, and Winston Churchill. "You are making history, madam," Churchill told her. While male correspondents looked on, Rinehart was getting the stories. Her articles increased the *Post's* circulation by 50,000 and her subsequent volume, *Kings, Queens and Pawns*, was praised as a great and original war book.

Returning to the United States a celebrity, Rinehart continued her crime writing, reworking *The Circular Staircase* into a drama entitled *The Bat*. When she asked her producer what he thought of the idea of a play that kept the audience in suspense until almost the drop of the curtain, his casual reply, "it would be worth a million," underestimated the result. Hailed as the best mystery play ever seen in New York, *The Bat* eventually grossed over nine million dollars and spawned several films.

In 1921, the Rineharts moved to Washington where Dr. Rinehart worked for the government before retiring to become his wife's business manager. Murder and mayhem allowed the Rineharts to live extremely well. Their home, now the Zambian Embassy, had eight telephones and was pointed out by tour guides as belonging to "America's Mistress of Mystery." For a dozen years the Rineharts made the social rounds of the nation's capital, attending presidential dinners and entertaining diplomats.

Following her husband's death in 1932, Rinehart traded Massachusetts Avenue for Park Avenue in New York, where she could be close to her sons' new publishing firm, Farrar and Rinehart, Inc. Her luxurious 18-room apartment had antique furniture, fine paintings, and—some said—a ghost. The clicking of billiard balls was frequently heard even when the billiard room was empty.

By now, Rinehart was a national institution. Her 30 books had been translated into a dozen languages, and she claimed fans as diverse as Gertrude Stein and Herbert Hoover. To the average American, however, she was more than a good storyteller. *The New York Times* listed her as one of the 12 greatest women in the United States and people pointed to her success as proof that the American dream lived.

Shortly before her 70th birthday, Rinehart's life erupted into drama as chilling as any tale she ever wrote. At her summer house in Bar Harbor, Maine, her cook, who had been with her for 25 years, went berserk and tried to kill her. Luckily, his pistol misfired and after a chase during which he cornered her with two carving knives, he was finally knocked down and subdued by the gardener and the chauffeur. That night he hanged himself in jail. Several months later, a great fire raged over Mt. Desert Island, engulfing Bar Harbor and burning Rinehart's house to the ground.

It seemed like a time for endings, but Rinehart, as indomitable as ever, picked up the pieces and continued. She completed two more books and a revision of *My Story*, her bestselling autobiography, before she died quietly in her sleep in 1958.

Suggested Reading:

Jan Cohn: *Improbable Fiction: The Life of Mary Roberts Rinehart*
Mary Roberts Rinehart: *My Story*

Anne Royall

Journalist

b. June 11, 1769 Baltimore, Maryland
d. October 1, 1854 Washington, D.C.
Congressional

I never had a lesson in writing having been raised in the Wilds of the West amongst the Indians till I was grown; I merely learned to scrawl as fancy led me.

Anne Royall, 1822

Imagine a crusty old woman not much taller than a powder keg. Dress her in a hoop skirt and bonnet, give her a pen and a sense of duty. Throw in equal portions of Rona Barrett and Jack Anderson, a sense of humor and a volatile temper, and you have America's first woman journalist, Anne Newport Royall.

No one knows for sure, but by her own account Anne Newport was kidnapped as a child and raised by Indians in the "Wilds of the West"—probably western Pennsylvania. In 1797 she married William Royall, a wealthy Virginia farmer 20 years her senior. The alliance sat poorly with his relatives who considered Anne a backwoods peasant; and in 1823, a full ten years after her husband's death, they managed to strip her of any inheritance on grounds of adultery.

Fifty-four, widowed and penniless, Anne Royall resolved to earn a living publishing accounts of her travels throughout the United States. To pay her way, she "subscriptioneered" book purchases and then delivered the finished products personally. These impressions remain a valuable record of early 19th-century American life. Mrs. Royall was prone to writing acid portraits of people she didn't like, which sometimes resulted in violent replies. She was on various occasions beaten with a cowskin, horsewhipped, chased by a mob, and tossed down a flight of stairs, breaking her leg.

Seeking a pension as a soldier's widow, Royall moved to Washington in 1829 and was almost immediately at war with a

Presbyterian group that worshiped next door. Fed up with her feisty behavior, they sought to have her tried as a "common scold." Whether such a law existed was unimportant, the main objective was a public comeuppance for this "holy terror." The trial was a great social success, attracting the likes of Francis Scott Key, Secretary of War John Eaton, and publisher Joseph Gales. A phrenologist (one who studies skull shape as an indicator of character and mental faculties) pronounced the defendant "beyond a doubt partially insane." A defense witness was forced to agree with the prosecution that he had been slandered by Mrs. Royall: "She has said . . . that I am very clever—and to that I make no objections; but she adds—'and a very exemplary man.' Now that's slander!" Anne herself suggested that the whole event be immortalized in oils on the walls of the Capitol rotunda.

The trial may have been a source for much local amusement, but Anne was convicted nonetheless. The traditional sentence, a public ride on a ducking stool, was considered too harsh by the prosecutor. Feeling that a person deserved some privacy while taking a cold bath, he accepted a ten-dollar fine in lieu of the dunking. Two reporters for the *National Intelligencer* paid the fine as a gesture in defense of a free press.

Believing that a newspaper should "educate people to respect, maintain and defend free government," Royall began publishing a weekly paper, *Paul Pry*, in 1831, in which she pursued government reform in a spirited editorial style that frequently bordered on slander. After five years, *Paul Pry* was nearly bankrupt, so she scrapped it and started over with *The Huntress*, which survived until her death in 1854. Royall advocated justice for the American Indian, separation of church and state, and states' choice on slavery, predicting 30 years before the Civil War the dissolution of the Union. She peddled her papers throughout Washington practicing subscription through intimidation. Refusal to subscribe could bring a barrage of four-letter character judgments and a blunt personal assault in the next issue. Those who did buy might receive kind treatment from her pen, although she never let relationships cloud her perception of the issues; her political viewpoint was fiercely independent.

Anne Royall's enemies were plentiful, but she counted John Quincy Adams among her close friends. Adams wrote of her:

She is a virago errant in enchanted armor, redeeming herself from the cramps of poverty by the notoriety of her eccentricities, the insane fear-

lessness of her attacks on public characters. She was the terror of politicians, and especially of congressmen. I can see her now tramping through the halls of the old Capitol, her keen eye searching every passerby, her thin lips firmly set like that of an old man, an old woman, yet possessed of great industry and indomitable will. She possessed without a doubt the most remarkable memory I have ever known.

A favorite story has Royall surprising President Adams while he swam naked in the Potomac River, sitting on his clothes and refusing to leave until he revealed his stand on a touchy issue. The story is in perfect keeping with her style and character, but probably never happened. Adams was no longer president when Royall moved to the capital in 1829.

In her last years Royall struggled to keep herself and her paper afloat, often publishing pleas for payment from her subscribers. A circulation of about four hundred left little room for tardy dues. She was also reduced to begging, but was too proud to call it that. She had been keeping a watchful eye on the federal government for 23 years when she died, at age 85, in her home which stood on the present grounds of the Library of Congress. Anne Royall's point of view may not have been read by all the powerful people of her day, but it is a compliment to her tenacious bit of democratic spirit that the Library of Congress has seen fit to preserve each issue of her papers in its Rare Book Collection.

Anne Royall Sampler

Our course will be a straightforward one. . . The same firmness which has ever maintained our pen will be continued. To this end, let it be understood that we are of no party. We will neither oppose nor advocate any man for the Presidency. The welfare and happiness of our country is our politics. To promote this we shall oppose and expose all and every species of political evil. . . We shall patronize merit of whatever country, sect or politics. We shall advocate the liberty of the Press, the liberty of Speech, and the liberty of Conscience. The enemies of these bulwarks of our common safety, as they have shown none, shall receive no mercy at our hands.

. . . Let all pious Generals, Colonels and Commanders of our army and navy who make war upon old women beware. . . Let all pious ladies who hawk pious tracts into young gentlemen's rooms beware, and let all old bachelors and old maids be married as soon as possible.

from first issue of "Paul Pry,"
December 3, 1831

We are bound to spread the news before the people, true or false.

The man who would oppress an aged female, by depriving her of the means of procuring bread, would rob his grandmother.

(Of Amos Kendall, Postmaster General, whom she accused of suppressing delivery of her paper)

How to meet a Creditor: If you see your creditor at a distance, walk boldly up to him, hope his rheumatism is better, and, before he can remind you that you faithfully promised to pay him three weeks ago, hint to him that he has neglected sending in your account, and that you must have it by the twenty-fifth of next month. Tell him to call for the amount on that day. You need not be at home, for he won't come.

We have to say this of the Constitution, that if it allows interested men to vote great sums of money out of other people's pockets into their own, it is very deficient.

Suggested Reading:

Sarah Harvey Porter: *The Life and Times of Anne Royall*
Bessie Rowland James: *Anne Royall's U.S.A.*

Phil Sheridan

Union General

b. March 6, 1831 Albany, New York?
d. August 5, 1888 Nonquitt, Massachusetts
Arlington

And there, through the flush of morning light
A steed as black as the steeds of night,
Was seen to pass as with eagle flight,
As if he knew the terrible need,
He stretched away with utmost speed;
Hills rose and fell; but his heart was gay,
With Sheridan fifteen miles away.

from "Sheridan's Ride" by T. Buchanan Read

On October 19, 1864, Phil Sheridan's Army of
the Shenandoah was camped a dozen miles south of
Winchester, Virginia, at Cedar Creek. Uncharacteristically,
Sheridan was not with his men. He was in Winchester, on his
way back from consultations with Secretary of War Edwin M.
Stanton in Washington. Before dawn, he was awakened by an
aide who had heard the distant rumble of artillery. Sheridan
rode out of Winchester toward the sound of battle only to come
upon the appalling sight of his own army fleeing toward him in
a rout. Quickly, he ordered a cavalry brigade to form a line
across the valley and halt the chaotic retreat. As he continued
through his demoralized men toward the front, Sheridan
pointed forward and shouted "Come on back, boys! Give 'em
hell! We'll make coffee out of Cedar Creek tonight!" The sight
and sound of Sheridan charging ahead on his horse, cheering
and swearing, fired his army with new hope. By evening the
disaster of early morning had been turned into a rout of the
Confederates. It was Philip Henry Sheridan's grandest moment.
In time, artists and poets would give the day an air of triumphant myth, celebrating the stunning Union victory that followed "Sheridan's Ride."

All five feet, five inches of "Little Phil" Sheridan was combustible fighting man. The child of working class Irish immigrants, Sheridan did not know where he was born, at various times claiming Massachusetts, Albany, New York, and Somerset, Ohio as his birthplace. He grew up in Somerset and entered West Point in 1848. In 1851, an aristocratic, Southern upper-classman made insulting remarks about the young Ohioan's background. Sheridan responded by leveling a bayonet at the other cadet's chest. Later, Sheridan greeted the cadet with a flurry of punches that nearly got him expelled. Suspended for a year, he was graduated in 1853.

As a leader, Sheridan was sometimes criticized as being all infectious nerve with no tactical sense, but early in the Civil War he demonstrated his unique blend of guts and cunning. On July 1, 1862, Sheridan's garrison of 827 cavalry was attacked by five thousand Confederate troops at Booneville, Mississippi. Pressed by the larger force into a flee-or-be-killed predicament, Sheridan chose instead to fight back. He sent 90 cavalry around to the rear of the Confederate army, and at a prearranged time all of Sheridan's forces charged the center of the enemy line. Just as the last-ditch attack got under way, a train full of hay pulled into town. Sheridan galloped over to the engineer and told him to blow the train whistle loud and long, hoping to convince his men that reinforcements had arrived. The plan worked, and the outnumbered Union forces charged the Confederates wildly, thinking fresh troops were following right behind. Under attack from both front and rear, the rebels believed a huge Northern force was enveloping them. They panicked and fled, assuring 31-year-old Phil Sheridan of victory and a promotion to brigadier general.

Sheridan suffered with the rest of Rosecrans's army in the humiliation at Chickamauga, but rebounded to lead the Northern forces to an impressive victory at Missionary Ridge, near Chattanooga. In that battle, the Union army scaled a slope that was so steep the Confederates simply lit the fuses of cannonballs and rolled them down the hill at the enemy. As was his habit, Sheridan fought side by side with his troops in taking the ridge and then led the charge down the other side to capture General Bragg's headquarters.

In the summer of 1864, rebel General Jubal Early had come too close to attacking Washington for Union comfort. When he pulled back into the Shenandoah Valley, General Grant called on Sheridan to drive him out. Sheridan was given 40,000 men

Phil Sheridan. Credit: Library of Congress

and a two-word order from Grant: "Go in." In successive victories against Early, Sheridan pushed the Confederates south to Staunton. With most of Virginia's breadbasket—and Lee's primary supply source—in his control, Sheridan turned the army around, fanned it across the valley, and marched north, burning nearly everything to the ground. Only private homes were spared; the fall harvest was completely destroyed. Sheridan wrote, "I have destroyed over two thousand barns filled with wheat, hay, and farm implements, over 70 mills filled with flour and wheat . . . and have killed and issued to the troops not less than three thousand sheep." The devastation was so complete it was said a crow flying over the valley would need to pack rations in order to survive.

Even with the precious Shenandoah a smoldering wasteland, Early was unwilling to give up the fight. He followed Sheridan north and craftily planned the attack at Cedar Creek when Sheridan was summoned to Washington. But thanks to Sheridan, Early's army had found nothing to eat while marching north and was nearly starving when it routed the Yankees early that October morning. The rebels were too weak and hungry to press their advantage, and Sheridan knew it. Patiently, he organized his scattered army, and at four in the afternoon he sent a division under General George Armstrong Custer against Early's weary men. The rebel line broke easily, and by nightfall Sheridan's men were drawing water from Cedar Creek to make their coffee. The destruction of the Shenandoah Valley brought immediate results for Sheridan; through the winter it would take its toll on Lee's army and pave the way for the ultimate Union victory.

Joining up with Grant in spring 1865, Sheridan won a decisive battle at Five Forks, south of Richmond. One officer remembered that Sheridan went "dashing from one point of the line to another, waving his flag, shaking his fist, encouraging, threatening, praying, swearing—the very incarnation of battle." On April 7, Grant received this message from President Lincoln: "Gen. Sheridan says 'If the thing is pressed I think Lee will surrender.' Let the thing be pressed." Two days later Sheridan blocked Lee's westward escape, and the Civil War was over.

One of Lincoln's greatest problems during the Civil War was finding generals who could lead the Union armies to victory. Sheridan, along with Grant and Sherman, had solved that problem. After the war, he was made military governor of Louisiana and Texas, but his firm fighting hand was too harsh for administering Andrew Johnson's Reconstruction policies, so he was unleashed on the Plains Indians instead. A revered national hero, Sheridan succeeded Sherman as general-in-chief of the Army in 1883, and was promoted to full general shortly before his death in 1888.

Suggested Reading:

Richard O'Connor: *Sheridan, the Inevitable*
Edward J. Stackpole: *Sheridan in the Shenandoah*

John Philip Sousa

Composer, Bandmaster

b. November 6, 1854 Washington, D.C.
d. March 6, 1932 Reading, Pennsylvania
Congressional

Hurrah for the flag of the free!
May it wave as our standard forever,
The gem of the land and the sea,
The banner of the right.
Let despots remember the day
When our fathers with mighty endeavor
Proclaimed as they marched to the fray
That by their might and by their right
It waves forever!

chorus to "The Stars and Stripes Forever"

You can bring out the high-stepping drum major, baton-twirling majorettes, and the big bass drum. You can dress the band in gold-trimmed uniforms and line up the colorful floats. But without the vitality of a Sousa march, the parade will never be complete! The name John Philip Sousa is synonymous with holiday parades and he is as much the "March King" now as he was in his heyday. Actually, Sousa was equally famous as composer, conductor, and entertainer; and was instrumental in earning foreign respect for American music. Performing in sell-out concerts around the world, Sousa was a turn-of-the-century superstar.

A native of Washington, D.C., young Sousa was fascinated by the military marching bands that frequently passed through the capital during the Civil War. His own musical talents were evident early. Once a circus bandleader persuaded the 13-year-old Sousa to run away with the circus as a fiddler, but his father foiled the plan by enlisting him in the Marine Band the next morning.

In 1880, at the age of 26, Sousa became director of the Marine Band, which performed for the White House. The March

King transformed this lackluster outfit into a band in demand, revamping its repertoire and rehearsing it to perfection. Two of Sousa's best known marches, "The Washington Post" and "Semper Fidelis," date from this time.

Until 1892, Sousa sold his compositions to publishers outright. His asking price ranged from five to fifty dollars apiece; and since he had been reared under extremely modest financial circumstances, he was satisfied to be able to sell them at all. But when he discovered that one publisher had bought two instrument factories with royalties from his works, Sousa quickly changed his point of view. Needless to say, his marches were worth millions; and as a result of his own bad experiences in realizing a profit from his works, Sousa became a founding member of the first organization formed to protect composers' rights, the American Society of Composers, Authors and Publishers (ASCAP).

Sousa formed his own band in 1892. Over the next 39 years this concert band (it marched only seven times) traveled over a million miles and gave more than ten thousand performances. Comprised of many of the finest musicians in America, the Sousa Band succeeded in breaking a long-held European prejudice against American music and musicians in four tours of that continent.

Owing partly to Sousa's endearing qualities as a stage performer, the European tours were always memorable. During one concert in Wales, the weight of the 55 piece band caused part of the stage to collapse, tossing Sousa seven feet down into a tangle of music stands and splintered wood. Undaunted, the March King crawled out, bowed deeply, said "We will now continue," and after cheers from the audience, calmly finished the program.

While returning from another trip abroad, Sousa was captivated by the rhythm of an imaginary band playing in his head. Melodic themes unfolded, and the band kept repeating them throughout the voyage. "Perhaps you should be putting the melody down on paper," his wife told him. "It won't get away," he replied. As the ship steamed into New York past the Statue of Liberty, the new composition took its final shape. "I did not transfer a note of that music to paper while I was on the steamer," recalled Sousa, "but when we reached the shore, I set down the measures that my brain-band had been playing for me, and not a note of it has ever been changed." Titled "The Stars and Stripes Forever," it is perhaps the best known

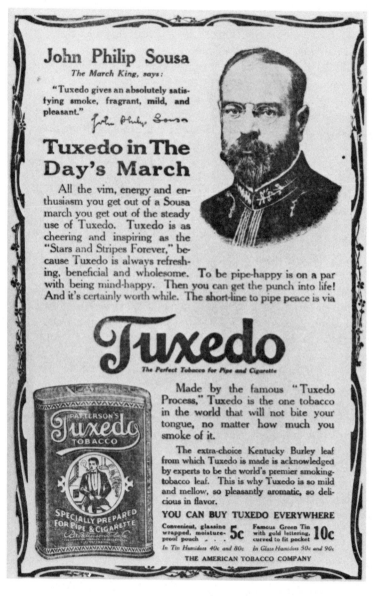

John Philip Sousa

The March King, says:

"Tuxedo gives an absolutely satisfying smoke, fragrant, mild, and
pleasant."

John Philip Sousa

Tuxedo in The Day's March

All the vim, energy and enthusiasm you get out of a Sousa
march you get out of the steady
use of Tuxedo. Tuxedo is as
cheering and inspiring as the
"Stars and Stripes Forever," because Tuxedo is always refresh-
ing, beneficial and wholesome. To be pipe-happy is on a par
with being mind-happy. Then you can get the punch into life!
And it's certainly worth while. The short-line to pipe peace is via

Tuxedo

The Perfect Tobacco for Pipe and Cigarette

Made by the famous "Tuxedo
Process," Tuxedo is the one tobacco
in the world that will not bite your
tongue, no matter how much you
smoke of it.

The extra-choice Kentucky Burley leaf
from which Tuxedo is made is acknowledged
by experts to be the world's premier smoking-
tobacco leaf. This is why Tuxedo is so mild
and mellow, so pleasantly aromatic, so deli-
cious in flavor.

YOU CAN BUY TUXEDO EVERYWHERE

Convenient, glassine
wrapped, moisture-
proof pouch . . . **5c**

Famous Green Tin
with gold lettering,
curved to fit pocket **10c**

In Tin Humidors 40c and 80c   *In Glass Humidors 50c and 90c*

THE AMERICAN TOBACCO COMPANY

*At one time happy to sell his compositions for as little as five dollars
apiece, John Philip Sousa eventually learned how to make the most of
his worth. This endorsement appeared in Washington's Evening Star
newspaper in 1915.* Credit: Peter Exton

melody in American music. When the rousing piece was performed in its early days, it caused one admirer to think of "the American eagle shooting arrows into the aurora borealis!"

Sousa composed and conducted in an energetic style intended to entertain. He worked hard to please his audiences and was rewarded with immense popularity. It was not unusual for 40,000 people to attend a Sousa concert, and at one performance the turnstile count was a record 153,000! In addition to his spirited marches, Sousa wrote comic operas, waltzes, suites, songs, and even found time for several novels and an autobiography. Although Sousa's Marine Band made some of the earliest recordings for the phonograph, he coined the term "canned music," fearing the new invention endangered live performance.

Sousa remained a celebrated figure throughout his life, active until the end. "If you hear that I have retired, you will know that I have died," he often joked. In fact, he died suddenly in Reading, Pennsylvania, only hours after a rehearsal. The only eulogy at his funeral was music. As the caisson started toward the cemetery, the Marine Band struck up Sousa's "Semper Fidelis" in dirge tempo.

Suggested Reading:

Ann M. Lingg: *John Philip Sousa*
Paul E. Bierley: *John Philip Sousa: American Phenomenon*
John Philip Sousa: *Marching Along: Recollections of Men, Women and Music*

Edwin M. Stanton

Lincoln's Secretary of War

b. December 19, 1814 Steubenville, Ohio
d. December 24, 1869 Washington, D.C.
Oak Hill

*While every honest heart rises in gratitude to God for the victories
which afford so glorious a guaranty of the national salvation, let it not
be forgotten that it is to Edwin M. Stanton, more than any other
individual, that these auspicious events are now due.*

Horace Greeley, 1865

Late one night at the height of the Civil War, a
government official came upon Secretary of War Edwin M.
Stanton in the halls of the War Department. Kneeling at his
feet were the mother, wife, and three children of an army des-
erter who had been condemned to die by firing squad. Hardly
able to speak through heaves of sobbing, they begged for the
man's life, but Stanton seemed unaffected by their pleas. Coldly
he told them, "The man must die." Without another word,
he disappeared into his office. The shaken official who witnessed the incident tells the rest: "My own heart was wrung
with anguish. It seemed to me that Mr. Stanton must be a de-
mon, the very incarnation of cruelty and tyranny. I was so
dazed that, forgetting myself, I followed Mr. Stanton into his office without rapping. I found him leaning over his desk, his
face buried in his hands and his heavy frame shaking with
sobs. 'God help me to do my duty,' he repeated, in a low wail
of anguish. This scene I shall never forget. I quickly and without noise withdrew, but not until I had seen a great light."

In the years since, not many people have seen the light of
Edwin McMasters Stanton. He is usually described as blunt,
humorless, and abrasive, a beefy troll of a man who attempted
to muscle control of whatever he needed to run the Union war
effort during the Civil War. It is true that Stanton would not be
found on a list of history's most charming personalities, but as
Lincoln's choice as Secretary of War during the greatest threat

to the survival of this nation, he was the right man for a terrible and largely unappreciated job. Extremely capable and self-confident, Stanton drafted, organized, armed, supplied, and directed an army that ballooned from 16,000 men in 1861 to over a million by the end of the war. And as the war dragged on, a desertion rate of one-third threatened to undermine the final victory. Firm action was Stanton's only recourse. "If the pyramids were upon my heart," he said, "the load would be light compared with what I have to bear." It was a time to steel the heart and save the Union.

A precocious youngster, Edwin Stanton started working in a Steubenville, Ohio, bookstore when he was 13, but was often so absorbed in reading that customers were left to fend for themselves. Before long, he had established a circulating library and charged ten cents for each book borrowed. A frustrated ex-girlfriend concluded that "he loved books better than girls."

Stanton became a lawyer in 1836. With an impressive string of courtroom successes behind him, by 1856 he was handling important government cases and moved his practice to Washington. He served briefly as Attorney General under James Buchanan; but when Abraham Lincoln was elected, Stanton returned to private practice. However, his ardent belief in preserving the Union did not go unnoticed by Lincoln; and when the President needed a strong, assertive individual to manage the Northern armies, he rested his hopes on Edwin Stanton.

From the outset, Stanton was faced with a monumental task. Never before had the country been in need of so much manpower and supplies in so short a time. Stanton's ability to be decisive, albeit sometimes rude as well, was indispensable amid the ensuing confusion. He created the army, and to protect it, he assumed control of the telegraph system, which had formerly been open to use by almost anyone, Confederate spies included. He appropriated all locomotives for government use. Halting a drain on the U.S. treasury, Stanton canceled all purchases of munitions and supplies from Europe. The bold move paid off as Northern factories and shops sprang up to meet the demand.

Stanton frequently incurred the wrath of his field generals by meddling in their campaign strategies. But his singleminded purpose—to win the war—governed his actions. When Rosecrans suffered an overwhelming defeat at the battle of Chickamauga, Stanton acted within hours to aid him. He took

Disliked by many, respected by most, Edwin M. Stanton has long been overlooked as a hero of the Civil War. Credit: Library of Congress

23,000 troops from the Army of the Potomac and within a week moved them six hundred miles to stem the rebel offensive. By holding eastern Tennessee, the Union Army was able to regroup and push into Georgia, setting the stage for Sherman's burning of Atlanta and march to the sea.

During the war Stanton steadfastly avoided any action that would suggest a recognition of the seceding states as a separate country. When the Confederates proposed an exchange of prisoners on "the frontier," Stanton refused, because the term implied a border between two countries. Late in 1864, Jefferson Davis sent a message to President Lincoln expressing an interest in bringing "peace to the two countries." Lincoln was encouraged, but Stanton held firm: "There are not two countries," he told the President, "and there never will be two countries.

Tell Davis that, if you treat for peace, it will be for this one country. Negotiations on any other basis are impossible." Lincoln rejected Davis's overture.

Stanton began his term as Secretary of War thinking of Lincoln's administration as an exercise in "imbecility," but by war's end he had gained a profound respect for his commander-in-chief, who had also become a close friend. When John Wilkes Booth shot Lincoln five days after Lee's surrender, the celebration of their triumph in saving the Union turned abruptly to sorrow. It was Stanton, his cold, hard exterior broken into streams of tears, who looked out from the room where Lincoln had just died and said, "He now belongs to the ages."

When the new president, Andrew Johnson, retained Stanton as Secretary of War, neither man could have known that they would engage in a power struggle that would lead to the first and only impeachment of a U.S. president. Johnson was not a Lincoln, and Stanton attempted to exploit his weaknesses by usurping control of the army now occupying the South. In August 1867, Johnson asked Stanton to resign, but Stanton refused, citing the recent Tenure of Office Act that protected cabinet officers from being fired by the president. In January 1868, Johnson suspended Stanton, but the Senate would not approve the President's action. Finally, in February, Johnson decided to test the legality of the Tenure of Office Act by dismissing Stanton outright. Stanton responded by barricading himself in his office and placing a guard outside while the Senate began impeachment proceedings against Johnson. On May 26, 1868, more than three months after Stanton had holed up in the War Department, Johnson survived the impeachment by one vote. Stanton resigned the same day.

History has not been kind to Edwin Stanton. His silly behavior during Johnson's impeachment is often recounted while his role in the Civil War is overlooked. True, Stanton was a headstrong official who precipitated the impeachment of a president. But he was also, and more importantly, an active defender of an indivisible United States and an unsung hero of the Civil War.

Suggested Reading:

Benjamin P. Thomas and Harold M. Hyman: *Stanton: The Life and Times of Lincoln's Secretary of War*
Fletcher Pratt: *Stanton: Lincoln's Secretary of War*

William Howard Taft

27th President

> b. September 15, 1857 Cincinnati, Ohio
> d. March 8, 1930 Washington, D.C.
> Arlington

Oscar Wilde said the only thing worse than being talked about is being forgotten, and "Big Bill" Taft might well agree. More often ignored than criticized, the amiable successor to the hero of San Juan Hill had a tough act to follow. Teddy Roosevelt's Rough Rider philosophy had brought new excitement and prestige to the presidency. Unlike Roosevelt, Taft believed in a government of laws, not men; his route to the White House was via the courtroom and administrative posts, not the political stump. Though he was handpicked to carry on Roosevelt's policies, he was no pawn and finally incurred Roosevelt's wrath. But if Taft was not as colorful as his predecessor, in his own gregarious and good-natured way he accomplished much toward streamlining the government and bringing a genuine warmth to the White House.

Originally from Ohio, Taft was educated at Yale and Cincinnati Law College. He held several legal and teaching posts until 1900 when President McKinley appointed him Civil Governor of the Philippines, where he introduced needed reforms and limited self-rule. From 1904–1908 he served as Teddy Roosevelt's Secretary of War before being chosen as the President's successor.

Legend has it that one night when Taft and his wife were visiting the Roosevelts at the White House, Teddy closed his eyes and began chanting:

I am the seventh son of a seventh daughter. I have clairvoyant powers. I see a man standing before me weighing about 350 pounds. There is something hanging over his head. I cannot make out what it is; it is hanging by a slender thread. At one time it looks like the Presidency—then again it looks like the Chief Justiceship.

"The Presidency!" cried Mrs. Taft. "The Chief Justiceship!" yelled her husband. In the end it was both. But Taft never enjoyed being president; his happiest years were spent on the Supreme Court.

The election of 1908 pitted the reluctant Taft against the aggressive William Jennings Bryan. Taft refused to engage in mud-slinging and his straightforward honesty won the voters. He did not accept campaign contributions from large corporations and, while completely temperate himself, favored a local option on the issue of prohibition. About all Bryan could criticize was Taft's ardent love of golf and his Unitarianism. When the votes were counted, Taft seemed chagrined. "I pinch myself every little while to make myself realize that it is all true," he told a friend. "I feel just a bit like a fish out of water." Maybe he was.

As President, Taft let Roosevelt's Big Stick gather dust. His foreign policy—tagged "Dollar Diplomacy"—favored peaceful overseas investment rather than military intervention. At home, he continued Roosevelt's trust-busting and conservation policies, but he moved too slowly for the Republican progressives and they soon deserted him.

Taft's size may have influenced his comfortable style. At 5'11" and over three hundred pounds, he was the country's biggest president ever. A special bathtub had to be installed at the White House to accommodate him. He was said to be the most polite man in Washington, graciously giving his seat on a streetcar to three women. The story is told that as a young lawyer Taft visited a small town. When ready to leave, he found that the next train didn't usually stop at the town. Thinking fast, he asked the station master to wire the train: "Will No. 7 stop here for a large party?" As he climbed aboard, Taft grinned at the conductor and patted his belly: "You can go ahead; I am the large party."

One of Taft's major contributions to government is often overlooked. Nowadays, the president and congress try manfully to balance the budget, but before Taft few people thought about a comprehensive financial plan for the government. After taking office, Taft called on department heads to prepare estimates for the next fiscal year, stressing that they cut costs whenever possible. These estimates were then checked by the President and his Cabinet, and for the first time in American history a comprehensive annual budget was drawn up. In 1912, Taft pointed out that the United States was the only great nation operated without a budget, and recommended an annual budget be formally adopted. Although Congress did nothing, many of Taft's

William Howard Taft on the golf links, enjoying his favorite pastime.
Credit: Library of Congress

ideas for improving the management of government finances
were eventually put into practice.

A more visible contribution was Mrs. Taft's introduction of
cherry trees into the capital. Nellie Taft loved flowers. She had
seen the cherry blossom festivals in Japan and decided Washington needed a grove of the trees. The mayor of Tokyo offered
two thousand saplings, but when these arrived infected with
scale they had to be destroyed. On hearing this the mayor
joked, "I believe your first president set the example of de-
stroying cherry trees, didn't he?" A replacement batch thrived,
and today Washington's cherry blossoms attract thousands of
visitors each spring.

The Tafts led an informal life in Washington. They had the last cow kept at the White House and the first automobile. The President liked nothing better than to drive around the city in the cool of the evening before bed.

The closing months of the Taft administration were marred by an increasingly bitter quarrel between the President and Theodore Roosevelt. Taft had turned out to be less progressive than Roosevelt had expected, and in 1912 Teddy again threw his hat into the ring for the Republican nomination. "The fight is on," he declared, "and I am stripped to the buff." At the convention, however, the political steamroller which had given Taft the nomination in 1908 flattened Roosevelt. Hurt by his rejection, Roosevelt took his delegates and formed the Bull Moose Party, thus splitting the Republicans. In the three-cornered election that followed, Woodrow Wilson and the Democrats swept to victory.

Taft seemed more relieved than disappointed. "Politics makes me sick," he complained in his private correspondence. And to Wilson entering the White House he warned, "This is the loneliest place in the world."

After a stint teaching law at Yale, "Smiling Bill" was delighted when President Harding appointed him Chief Justice of the Supreme Court in 1921, making him the only man to serve as head of the country and head of the court. His geniality earned him the praise of Justice Oliver Wendell Holmes, Jr. who called Taft's first year the most pleasant he had experienced with the court.

One of Taft's dreams was to move the Supreme Court from the Old Senate chamber in the Capitol into its own building. Although he didn't live to see this happen, before he died in 1930 Taft managed to secure congressional approval for today's magnificent Supreme Court building.

The memorable accomplishments of his administration were few, but Taft brought much-needed warmth and openness to the presidency. When he left the White House, Will Rogers summed up his term:

It's great to be great but it's greater to be human. He was our great human fellow because there was more of him to be human. We are parting with three hundred pounds of solid charity to everybody, and love and affection for all his fellow men.

Suggested Reading:

Judith Icke Anderson: *William Howard Taft: An Intimate History*

Apotheosis of Washington. *Although he declined to be king of the United States, George Washington was crowned in heaven by artists within a year of his death.* Credit: National Portrait Gallery

George Washington

First President

b. February 22, 1732 Pope's Creek, Westmoreland
County, Virginia
d. December 14, 1799 Mount Vernon, Virginia
Mount Vernon

Every school-child knows the story of the
young boy who could not tell a lie and admitted to an astonished father that he had chopped down a cherry tree. Most
people remember the story of young George throwing a silver
dollar across the Potomac. Then there's the story of Washington, at 14, nearly running away to sea. Indeed, a collection
of these tall tales would make entertaining reading; but the
true George Washington is as memorable as any myth he
inspired.

Born to a land-poor family near Fredericksburg, Virginia,
George had to struggle to become a Virginia gentleman. His father died when he was 11 and his formal education was
sketchy. Of the first six presidents, he was the only one not to
attend college. After several years as a surveyor, Washington
entered the militia and saw action in the French and Indian
War. At Braddock's Defeat, Washington had four bullets punc-
ture his coat and two horses shot from under him and nevertheless stayed in command of his troops, allowing one-third
of them to escape ambush.

Following the resignation of his commission in 1759, Washington married Martha Custis, one of the richest widows in Virginia, and settled down as a tobacco planter at Mount Vernon.
Though the marriage was not passionate, it was happy. It also
gave Washington prestige and financial security. Many observers considered Martha and George the perfect couple. Washington affectionately called Martha "Patsy" and wore a locket
containing a picture of her around his neck; Martha privately
referred to George as her "old man." Though he was already
being hailed as the "Father of His Country" during his lifetime,
in 40 years of marriage George and Martha produced no children. A number of biographers believe a bout with smallpox at
age 19 may have left Washington sterile.

In 1775, Washington again found himself in uniform, this time as commander-in-chief of the colonial forces fighting the British. Although his troops suffered numerous defeats and Congress was too feeble to provide substantial aid, Washington was able to keep his army in the field and through determination, patience, and skill, inspire them to ultimate victory. When General Cornwallis surrendered at Yorktown in 1781, Washington reacted with his characteristic understatement calling it "an interesting event that may be productive of much good."

Despite his probably genuine desire to retire to Mount Vernon following the Revolution, Washington was unanimously elected president of the Constitutional Convention and later, when the Convention created the office of President of the United States, it was done specifically with Washington in mind.

As President, Washington realized the tremendous responsiblity he had to his country. At the time, there was no other elected head of state in Europe or the New World. "I walk on untrodden ground," he claimed, "there is scarcely any part of my conduct which may not hereafter be drawn into precedent."

Eager to set a high standard for the presidency, Washington virtually held court. In New York and Philadelphia, where the new federal government first met, he rented the best houses. He traveled in an expensive carriage, returned no calls, and shook hands with no one, preferring a formal bow. At receptions, he dressed in black velvet with yellow gloves, carried an ostrich plume in one hand and a sword in a white leather scabbard at his side. Those lucky enough to be invited to dine with the Washingtons complained that the elaborate meals were too solemn. All entertainment ended promptly at 9:00 P.M. when the President and "Lady Washington" went to bed.

Though on the surface the President often seemed cold and overly concerned with protocol, this was probably a way of masking his sensitive, shy nature. Washington was disciplined, but he was also very emotional. When bidding farewell to his officers after the Revolutionary War, his eyes filled with tears and he could barely speak. On learning of Benedict Arnold's treason, he shook with confusion and rage. When the Continental Congress met, Washington rarely spoke to the assembly, reserving his thoughts for more intimate after-hours discussions when he would forcefully present his ideas.

After declining a third term in office, Washington returned to

Mount Vernon and the life of a gentleman farmer. Martha loved the domestic routine which kept her "steady as a clock, busy as a bee, and cheerful as a cricket." Although he was not obsessed with death and was constantly making plans for the future of Mount Vernon, in July 1799, Washington filled 27 pages of his best water-marked paper with his will. On December 12, Washington rode out during a fierce winter storm to make his usual rounds of the farm. That night he woke with a chill which quickly developed into acute laryngitis. Two days later, after being bled several times, he died serenely, saying "I thank you for your attentions, but I pray you take no more trouble with me."

A week after Washington's burial at Mount Vernon, Congress made plans to move his remains to a tomb in the Capitol, a building he had laid the cornerstone for six years earlier. It was only after protests from Washington's relatives and the Virginia General Assembly that he was allowed to stay where he had wished, at his beloved plantation in the state of his birth. The empty tomb intended for Washington can still be seen in the basement of the Capitol.

Much of Washington's success must be credited to his personal bearing. At a time when the average American man was 5′ 7″ and weighed 150 pounds, Washington towered over his contemporaries. In his prime he carried himself with great dignity and poise, stood "straight as an Indian" at 6′ 2″, and weighed 220. He had enormous hands, and feet that required size 13 boots. Physically, Washington's sole complaint was the loss of his teeth which obliged him to wear uncomfortable dentures made of wood and elephant tusk. These greatly altered his facial expression, giving him sunken cheeks and an oddly set jaw. When Gilbert Stuart came to paint the President's portrait, he stuffed Washington's cheeks with cotton. The result is the noble image of George Washington known throughout the world today.

A Selection From
George Washington's Rules of Civility
(copied into a notebook when he was 16)

2. When in company, put not your hands to any part of the body not usually discovered.

7. Put not off your clothes in the presence of others, nor go out of your chambers half-dressed.

11. Shift not yourself in the sight of others nor gnaw your nails.

12. Shake not the head, feet or legs—roll not the eye—lift not one eyebrow higher than the other—wry not the mouth, and bedew no man's face with your spittle by approaching too near him when you speak.

13. Kill no vermin as fleas, lice, ticks, etc., in the sight of others. If you see any filth or thick spittle, put your foot dexterously upon it. If it be upon the clothes of your companions, put it off privately, and if it be upon your own clothes, return thanks to him who puts it off.

43. Do not express joy before one sick or in pain for that contrary passion will aggravate his misery.

53. Run not in the streets, neither go too slowly nor with mouth open. Go not shaking your arms. Kick not the earth with your feet. Go not upon the toes nor in a dancing fashion.

97. Put not another bit into your mouth til the former be swallowed—let not your morsels be too big for the jowls.

100. Cleanse not your teeth with the table cloth, napkin, fork, or knife, but if others do it, let it be done with a pick tooth.

110. Labor to keep alive in your breast that little spark of celestial fire called conscience.

Suggested Reading:

Noemie Emery: *Washington: A Biography*

James Thomas Flexner: *Washington, the Indispensable Man*

Woodrow Wilson

28th President

b. December 29, 1856 Staunton, Virginia
d. February 3, 1924 Washington, D.C.
Washington Cathedral

*Sometimes people call me an idealist. Well, that is the way I know I
am an American. America is the only idealistic nation in the world.*

Woodrow Wilson

The most highly educated man ever elected
President of the United States, Woodrow Wilson was guided by
an idealism that pumped new life into the goals of the founding
fathers. He made campaign promises with every intention of
keeping them and was a crusader on behalf of those who were
trampled by the stampede of industry. Wilson remains one of
the most admired men in our history, yet his refusal to compro-
mise his ideals cost him American membership in his dearest
dream, the League of Nations, and ultimately it hastened his
death.

Thomas Woodrow Wilson grew up in Virginia, Georgia, and
South Carolina. Memories of his childhood included images of
a South ravaged first by the Civil War and then by carpetbag-
gers' corruption. He also felt "the unspeakable joy of being
born and bred in a minister's family." His upbringing stressed
integrity, the good of public service and, of course, a devotion
to God and Christian teaching. By the time Tommie Wilson left
home, he had long been saying his nightly prayers kneeling at
his bedside, a practice he maintained throughout his adult life.

Wilson graduated from Princeton in 1879 and studied law at
the University of Virginia, but found it "as monotonous as . . .
Hash." He loved politics, however, and earned a Ph.D. in political science from Johns Hopkins University in 1885. His
doctoral thesis, Congressional Government, marked him as a
keen observer of how things really got done on Capitol Hill.

Freshly wed to Ellen Louise Axson, a woman who made him

221

the happiest man in "the Yewnighted States," Woodrow—he dropped his first name when he began publishing—took a teaching job at Bryn Mawr College. He also taught at Wesleyan College before being hired by Princeton, his alma mater, in 1890. Wilson's love of teaching and his clear and elegant treatment of his subjects made his classes the most popular on campus. His habit of always riding a bicycle to class further endeared him to the faculty and students alike.

A bicycle may not have been typical of college faculty, but everything else about Wilson was pure professor. His trademark was the pince-nez glasses perched on the ridge of a refined, angular nose. Lean, seemingly aloof and often intense, Wilson lamented that he appeared "a mere book-man." Although he possessed a lively wit and loved charades, storytelling, and mimicking funny people, Wilson would never shake that bookish image. In fact, he spent so much time writing that his right hand became unreliable with frequent cramping. Rather than cut his work load, Wilson taught himself to write left-handed and kept on going.

In 1902, Wilson was unanimously elected president of Princeton. In that position, he hoped to eliminate some of the elitism that characterized Princeton and other private schools, once going so far as to claim that Lincoln would have been a lesser president had he attended a private college. His attempts to open Princeton to the less privileged fueled the ire of the trustees, but the press took note, and portrayed Wilson as a defender of democracy against the rich.

In 1910, at the same time that a parting of the ways seemed best for Wilson and Princeton, the New Jersey Democratic machine needed a popular hero to run for governor. Wilson agreed to be the candidate. Once elected, he made it clear that he was no puppet of back-room political bosses. In his campaign he had promised to enact liberal reform measures. To everyone's surprise, he did exactly that, and even when both houses of the state legislature were under Republican control, the professor-governor still managed to continue his reform programs.

Political success in New Jersey brought Wilson national recognition, and with a well-timed nudge from William Jennings Bryan he was nominated for president in 1912—on the 46th ballot! He campaigned for a return to the democratic ideals of the past and for "the man who is knocking and fighting at the closed doors of opportunity." Fortunately for Wilson, President William Howard Taft and Teddy Roosevelt split the Republican

Presidential lovebirds Edith Bolling Galt and Woodrow Wilson. Note cupid at work in lower right corner. Credit: Library of Congress

vote, enabling him to win the election with fewer votes than Bryan had polled in a landslide loss in 1908.

As soon as he took office, Wilson pursued a policy of labor and business reforms. Boycotts and strikes were legalized and tariffs were lowered to promote competition. On the foreign front, Wilson had tense relations with Mexico, sending marines to occupy Vera Cruz and General John J. Pershing across the Rio Grande after the marauding Pancho Villa. Feeling guilty for the U.S. seizure of the Panama Canal Zone, he wanted to apologize to Colombia and pay them $25 million for the land, but the Senate would not agree to it. These concerns, however, were minor compared to developments in Europe. In 1914, World War I erupted and Wilson spent most of his presidency trying to end it.

On May 7, 1915, the British liner *Lusitania*, with 128 Americans on board, was sunk by a German submarine. Wilson tried to maintain U.S. neutrality, and succeeded long enough to win re-election with the slogan "he kept us out of war." But in April 1916, after more submarine attacks, the

United States declared war on Germany, and Wilson urged his countrymen to join him in the fight to "make the world safe for democracy."

The U.S. entry into the war tipped the scales against the Germans, and in October 1918, they accepted Wilson's famous "Fourteen Points" as the basis for treaty negotiations. Wilson's hopes for a lasting "peace without victory" rested with these points, which also introduced his concept of a "general association of nations" that would be a forum for settling future disputes. As the national leader most responsible for bringing an end to the hostilities, Wilson was hailed almost as a savior when he arrived in Europe for the Versailles Peace Conference.

Had Woodrow Wilson's life ended at that moment, he might have gone down in history as something of a saint, if not a savior. Instead, he watched as European leaders shredded his 14 points along lines of centuries-old grudges, saddling Germany with conditions that Wilson was certain would lead to an even more terrible war. Weary and disheartened, he returned to America having saved very little from his original plan, but hoping that his 14th point, the League of Nations, could rectify all the wrongs created at Versailles.

Before sailing for Europe, Wilson had not asked for any advice from the Senate, and when he came home, the snubbed legislators were not in a cooperative mood. They wanted changes in the treaty, but Wilson was determined not to have his ideals diluted any further. Unable to woo the Senate, an already exhausted Wilson took his case to the people. Traveling by train, he covered eight thousand miles in 22 days rallying support for the treaty and the league. But the strain was too much. He became desperately ill and had to cancel the rest of the tour. Realizing his crusade was over, Wilson broke down and wept freely. He couldn't bear to consider himself a quitter, and felt that he was abandoning the most important issue in modern history. Tears streaking his face, he could only say, "This is the biggest disappointment of my life!" Shortly after returning to Washington, he suffered a stroke.

In 1914, Wilson's first wife had died, leaving him a lonely and emotionally fragile widower. Family and friends hoped to find him a new wife, and in 1915, through his cousin, Wilson met Edith Bolling Galt, a widow who was also a direct descendant of Pocahontas. They fell in love like a pair of dazed teens and brightened the days of impending war with their storybook romance. Henry Adams, who lived across from the White

House on Lafayette Square, was among those charmed by their courtship. "You've no idea," he told a friend, "how sweet it is when they kiss each other out walking." In December of that year, Mrs. Galt became the new First Lady.

After Wilson's stroke in 1919, Edith hovered over her recuperating husband, allowing almost no one to see him. She screened everyone and everything that came his direction and acted as a relay between top officials and the President, disappearing behind closed doors and later emerging with her husband's response. Many congressional leaders doubted that Wilson was actually governing. His signature on bills was suspected as forgery. Edith insisted that changes in the State of the Union Address—in her handwriting—were at the direction of the President. Some officials were outraged that such a situation existed at the very highest level of government, calling Mrs. Wilson the "Presidentress" at the helm of a "petticoat government."

The whole affair came to a head when two senators, one from each party, demanded a meeting with Wilson to determine if he was capable of performing his duties. Under carefully planned conditions designed by Edith to give Wilson his best possible appearance, the two men spoke with the President until they were satisfied that he was in good mental and physical health and fit to run the country. Although Wilson gradually recovered enough to resume a regular schedule, doubts still persist about whether or not we had a woman president for several months.

Woodrow Wilson was awarded the Nobel Prize for his efforts toward world peace, but the toll was heavy. His body had collapsed and his spirit was crushed. He completed his term in office as a convalescent figure and then retired to a quiet residence in the city of Washington. When he died in 1924, the country lost its greatest leader since Lincoln. Today Wilson's dream, the League of Nations, survives in the forum we call the United Nations.

Woodrow Wilson Quoted

The example of America must be the example not merely of peace because it will not fight, but of peace because peace is the healing and elevating influence of the world and strife is not. There is such a thing as a man being too proud to fight. There is such a thing as a nation being so right that it does not have to convince others by force that it is right.

response to sinking of the Lusitania

America cannot be an ostrich with its head in the sand.

It is a fearful thing to lead this great peaceful people into war . . . but the right is more precious than peace, and we shall fight for the things which we have always carried nearest our hearts—for democracy, for the right of those who submit to authority to have a voice in their own government, for the rights and liberties of small nations, for a universal dominion of right by . . . a concert of free peoples. . .

declaring war on Germany

A general association of nations must be formed . . . for the purpose of affording mutual guarantees of political independence and territorial integrity to great and small states alike.

the Fourteenth Point

There will come sometime . . . another struggle in which not a few hundred thousand fine men from America will have to die, but many millions . . . to accomplish the final freedom of the peoples of the world.

1919

Suggested Reading:

Arthur Walworth: *Woodrow Wilson*

The Unknown Soldiers

Although *Milestones into Headstones* is a book of biography, we would like to pay tribute to a group of Americans whose life stories we will never know: the Unknown Soldiers.

The Tomb of the Unknown Soldier in Arlington National Cemetery holds the remains of an unidentified American soldier from each of the wars we have fought in this century: World War I, World War II, the Korean War, and the Vietnam War. Also at Arlington, near the Custis-Lee Mansion, is a mass grave of 2,111 unknown Union soldiers of the Civil War. And at the Presbyterian Meeting House in Old Town, Alexandria (316 S. Royal St.), rest the remains of an unknown veteran of the Revolutionary War.

These Unknowns, from six wars, represent more than a million soldiers who fought and died for their country. Most of them were young.

In 1755, when he was only 23, George Washington survived the slaughter of Braddock's Defeat with four bullet holes in his coat. What if one had found his heart?

In 1862, 21-year-old Oliver Wendell Holmes, Jr. miraculously recovered from a bullet that had pierced his neck at Antietam. He had earlier survived a bullet through his chest.

In 1943, a Japanese destroyer sank PT-109 in the south Pacific. One of the survivors was 26-year-old John F. Kennedy.

Washington, Holmes, Kennedy. Three of many young soldiers who fought and came home to pursue their dreams. It isn't hard to imagine that among those who did not return were many talented men and women just like them.

We recognize the Unknowns, and all whom they represent, as great Americans. They gave up their dreams to make ours possible. If we think of them as potential Washingtons, Holmeses, and Kennedys, we can better appreciate their sacrifice, and our loss.

Getting There

Below are directions for getting to all the gravesite locations. Except for the graves of the Fitzgeralds and George Washington, they are all within the Capital Beltway and easy to find. In most cases, there is someone on hand who will be happy to show you where to go. We have included a checklist of names wherever multiple subjects are located, so you won't miss any that you want to see. It's a good idea to call ahead to make sure of the hours when each place is open.

Arlington National Cemetery
Arlington, Virginia 22211
(703)545-6700

Located directly across the Potomac from the Lincoln Memorial. You can go by car or subway. Cars are not allowed within the cemetery, but tour buses can help you get around. Get detailed directions on a cemetery map at the information booth.

Bennett	Holmes	Pershing
Bradley	Ingersoll	Powell
Bryan	John Kennedy	Ream
Byrd	Robert Kennedy	Reed
Clem	Louis	Rinehart
Donovan	Marshall	Sheridan
Doubleday	Murphy	Taft
Evers	Newcomb	Civil War Unknowns
Hammett	Peary	Tomb of Unknown Soldier

Congressional Cemetery
1801 E Street, S.E., Washington, D.C. 20003
(202)543-0539

Take Independence Avenue to 18th Street, S.E. Turn south and continue straight ahead to cemetery. Ask at gatehouse for cemetery map.

Brady	Hoover	Royall
Gales	Johnson	Sousa
Gerry	Pushmataha	

Glenwood Cemetery
2219 Lincoln Road, N.E., Washington, D.C. 20002
(202)667-1016

From North Capitol Street, bear right onto Lincoln Road and follow north to cemetery gate. Directions and a history of the cemetery are available in the office.

Brumidi	Gardner	Leutze

House of the Temple
1733 16th Street, N.W., Washington, D.C. 20009
(202)232-3579

At 16th and S Streets, N.W. Take a tour and have the guide explain the unique decorations.

Pike

Ivy Hill Cemetery
2823 King Street, Alexandria, Virginia 22303
(703)549-7413

Follow King Street (Rt. 7) west from the Masonic Temple to light at Janney's Lane. Cemetery is just ahead on the right. Ask for directions at the gatehouse.

von Braun

Mount Vernon
Mount Vernon, Virginia 22121
(703)780-2000

Take George Washington Memorial Parkway south through Alexandria (you are temporarily on Washington Street) to Mount Vernon. Fee.

Washington

Oak Hill Cemetery

30th and R Streets, N.W., Washington, D.C. 20007
(202)337-2835

At the top of 30th Street in Georgetown. Ask at the office.

Eaton   Payne   Stanton
Joyce

Presbyterian Meeting House

316 S. Royal Street, Alexandria, Virginia 22314
(703)549-6670

Take George Washington Memorial Parkway south to Old Town, Alexandria. The Parkway becomes Washington Street. Turn left at Prince Street. Go three blocks, turn right on Royal. Church ahead two blocks on right.

Unknown Veteran of Revolutionary War

Rock Creek Cemetery

Rock Creek Church Road & Webster Street, N.W., Washington, D.C. 20011
(202)829-0585

Follow North Capitol Street through Soldier's Home to Harewood Road. Turn left. Cemetery is straight ahead. Administration office to right of entrance has map and directions.

Adams

St. Mary's Church

Viers Mill Road, Rockville, Maryland 20852
(301)424-5550

Take Rockville Pike (Rt. 355) north to intersection with Viers Mill Road (Rt. 586). Churchyard is on the right. Marker is about twenty yards opposite back end of church.

Fitzgeralds

Washington Cathedral

Massachusetts & Wisconsin Avenues, N.W., Washington, D.C. 20016
(202)537-6200

Entrance on Wisconsin Avenue. Ask at information desk inside.

Dewey   Sullivan
Keller   Wilson

About the Authors

Peter Exton Credit: Ellen Blaisdell   Dorsey Kleitz Credit: Meredith Ricker

Ever since their high school days together in Arlington, Virginia, Peter Exton and Dorsey Kleitz had suspected that some fascinating biographies might be found beneath the famous-name graves of Washington, D.C. With *Milestones Into Headstones* they have confirmed that hunch, unearthing 50 thoroughly entertaining, informative life stories.

Mr. Exton, who graduated from Schiller University in Heidelberg, Germany, and spent many years in the capital area as a songwriter and club performer, is continuing his research and writing on historical subjects.

Mr. Kleitz is a graduate of Bard College and the University of Virginia. He has served in the Peace Corps in Africa, taught English in Saudi Arabia, and has published a number of travel articles and poems. He now teaches at the University of New Hampshire.